T0209944

Where do YOU want to go?

LAYTON PANG

WestBow
PRESS®
A DIVISION OF THOMAS NELSON
& ZONDERVAN

All scripture quotations are taken from The Holy Bible, New International Version®, NIV® Copyright © 1973, 1978, 1984, 2011 by Biblica, Inc.® Used by permission. All rights reserved worldwide.

WestBow Press books may be ordered through booksellers or by contacting:

WestBow Press
A Division of Thomas Nelson & Zondervan
1663 Liberty Drive
Bloomington, IN 47403
www.westbowpress.com
844-714-3454

ISBN: 979-8-3850-1110-0 (sc)
ISBN: 979-8-3850-1111-7 (hc)
ISBN: 979-8-3850-1112-4 (e)

Library of Congress Control Number: 2023920532

Print information available on the last page.

WestBow Press rev. date: 11/21/2023

Dedication

To my family and friends who have loved and supported me all my life, especially my Dad, Mom, sister, and brother. Without you, I would never have learned to love God and my life would never have been this great. I love all of you very much! This book is also dedicated to anyone who is not sure what to believe or where to go for help regarding this life and what happens after we leave this world. I hope this book encourages you to find Faith in the Lord and trust in Him for your eternal salvation. Even if you don't choose that path, I appreciate you for taking the time to read this book and hope it encourages you to live your life the best that you can. God Bless!

Index of Inspirations

Welcome

Thanks for taking time to read this book. I would like to start by saying that I am an Architect and not a professional writer, so I apologize in advance for any writing mistakes. Let me tell you a little bit about myself and the reason I decided to write this book. I was born and raised as a Catholic Christian, and I went to Church with my Family every Sunday. I have always believed in Jesus Christ and tried to live as best as I could in accordance with my upbringing and understanding of God. As I have grown older, several moments in my life have heightened my view on my relationship with God.

The only sure thing in life is that someday it will come to an end. No matter how good or bad you think your life is or how healthy you think you are, we all know that our time on earth is temporary. The loss of my Father in 2010 came much sooner than I was prepared for, and I had no idea how I would cope with that. He was such an important part of my life and a faithful man of Christ. I knew for sure that he was in Heaven and that if I wanted to see him again, that is where he would be. I also needed to find a way to handle losing the best man I had ever known. I prayed and asked God to guide me like He always had, and His answer was strong and clear to me. God called me to Him, not in death but in life, and it started with His Word, the Bible. I had heard and read scriptures during Church and Sunday school, but I had never read the Bible myself. My girlfriend had given me a beautiful Bible, and I decided to read it in its entirety and let God speak to me through His words.

I read a little bit every day, and it took me about a year to read every book from Genesis through Revelation (I am a slow reader). The Bible is the greatest book ever written; however, it is not like a normal book that you start at the beginning and read through until you get to the end. The Bible consists of the Old Testament and New Testament, with books in each having God's Word and guidance. The Old Testament chronicles the beginning of creation and humankind's relationship with God before the birth of Christ. The New Testament records the birth of Jesus Christ and takes us through His crucifixion and triumph over death. I asked God into my heart and read each book in whatever order He guided me. The more that I read, the more I wanted to read, and eventually it wasn't just a way to cope with the loss of my Father but the way I wanted to live my life. That was in 2010, and I continue to read the Bible every day with the help of a wonderful guide called *Our Daily Bread*.

Even though I go to Church and read the Bible every day, I am the first to admit that I am very flawed and still need to make a lot of improvements in my thoughts and behavior. We all need help at some point in our lives, and every task or journey has a starting point. Funny thing is that when we think we are making progress in something, we might find out that we were only preparing to get started. I have been blessed with a great life; however, I want to honor God and do more with His blessings. Many incidents and moments in my life have inspired me to write this book; however, I have not had the discipline to complete it. I started writing down thoughts and notes around 2014, shortly after the passing of one of my best friends, whom you will read about later. When you read this, you can figure out how long it took me to complete this book (procrastination is one of my flaws). I try to live every day to honor God, and this book is my written testimony and proclamation to Jesus!

I am hoping this book helps you see things from a positive perspective. It is not a fire-and-brimstone, finger-pointing rant against nonbelievers; rather it is an invitation to everyone to reflect on their lives and consider and embrace the love and joy Jesus Christ has for you. I am hoping this book has you consider how you want to live your life and where you want to spend eternity when your time on earth is over. So thanks again for joining me, and let's get started!

A Simple Question

All of us have asked or been asked, "Where do you want to go?" It is a simple question with a very wide range of implications. If the question pertains to lunch or dinner, it might not have much influence on your life. If the question is about choosing a vacation spot or college, it would carry much more weight. Deciding where you work and live as an adult will definitely impact your life. All of these examples vary to a degree, and we make choices throughout our lives, but what about after? No matter what your religion or faith is, or even if you have none, we can all agree that at some point in time, we will no longer be alive on this earth. Time is undefeated in this world, and everyone's physical body has or will expire. My question to you is when your time comes, where do YOU want to go? I am not asking where you *think* you will go, but where do you *want* to go? If you want to be reincarnated and come back as an eagle or a dog, then good luck with that; however, if you want to go to Heaven, then you need to consider how you will get there.

I have been to many funeral services honoring loved ones who have passed. At every one of these events, thoughts and prayers are focused on two things: (1) how special and loved that person was while alive and with us, and (2) although the person will be missed, we can take solace in that they have passed on to a better place. I do not know where that "better place" is or what that means to other religions or beliefs. I do know that for Christians that better place is Heaven—a place God created for His loved ones to spend eternity with Him after leaving their earthly bodies. When you reflect on loved ones who have passed, I am sure you wish the best for them. Anything created by humankind cannot compare to what God creates, so I can't imagine anything better than being in Heaven. My simple question to you again is where do *you* want to go? If your answer is Heaven, then you have taken the first step to get there. You must choose a destination before you get anywhere. With no destination, you are just wandering around. Once you decide where your destination is, then you have to figure out how to get there. There are two basic principles that determine where we arrive in our travels (physically or metaphorically): (1) the correctness of the directions and (2) how well we follow those directions. Think about the last time you asked someone for directions or planned a trip you were going to take. It starts with the destination, which is then followed by directions, procedures, or instructions. Once you have that information, you need to take proper steps. If the directions are wrong or you don't follow them correctly, it makes it much more difficult (and sometimes impossible) to reach your desired destination.

The principles of directions and following them correctly are not just limited to travel but apply to daily operations as well. Think of how many things in your life need directions or instructions. Something as simple as opening a pill bottle comes with directions/instructions. Imagine how difficult it would be to put together DIY (do-it-yourself) furniture or toys without the proper instructions. The easier (or closer) the destination, the simpler the directions are and the greater the chance at arriving where you planned. Some destinations or goals are much more complex and results are not assured. Let's use college as an example. If a high schooler chooses a college they would like to attend after graduating, the student has many steps to take just to apply. Every step comes with directions, and the student needs to follow them properly to even qualify to be accepted. Even if the student goes through the process and follows all the directions correctly, they are still not guaranteed the desired outcome, but the student at least has a chance. Sometimes a decision or judgment comes from others; however, if that student did not follow directions and the application never gets to the school, then it is certain that they won't get accepted. The point is, after obtaining proper directions, we need to put in the effort to follow them correctly, and nothing should be taken for granted.

Many times in life we do our best to put ourselves where we want to be, whether that is a physical location (like Hawaii), a financial situation (rich and wealthy), a physical condition (healthy and in shape), or an emotional state (happy and content). Sometimes we get there, sometimes we fall short, and sometimes we decide the desired result is not worth the effort. Whenever you come to that realization, you will have the opportunity make changes, either in your destination or your efforts. That is the biggest difference between what we do in this world and if we get to Heaven after our time on earth. If your desire is to spend eternity in Heaven, then you need to follow the right directions while you are alive to get there. We never know when our time is up, and we won't get a second chance to do the right things after we pass away. That is why it is so important to not just get the directions on how to get to Heaven, but to follow them so that we do not get lost along the way. We need to take this action as soon as possible because you never know when your time is up on this journey.

As I mentioned earlier, if you want to get somewhere, two things determine if you get to your desired destination: (1) the source and accuracy of the information, and (2) how well you follow those directions. You need both to be correct to be successful in your journey. If your answer to the question "where do you want to go (after death)?" is Heaven, then your next question should be "how do I get there?" There are so many articles, shows, books, religions, and other venues declaring their ways; however, it all comes down to one simple but all powerful entity—God. If you are a faithful Christian and believer in God, you know what I am talking about. If not, then allow me to explain.

Heaven is a place God has prepared for us to spend eternity with Him. There is only one God and only one Heaven, so you can take solace in knowing the absolute beauty of His plan for us and the oneness that this plan maintains. It all begins with *faith*. The dictionary defines faith as complete trust or confidence in something or someone without proof. The Bible describes Faith similarly:

> Now faith is being sure of what we hope for
> and certain of what we do not see.
> (Hebrews 11:1)

We all have or show faith in things, regardless of religion or any other belief. Adults know the term "faithful" regarding romantic relationships, and many children "believe" in Santa Claus. These are just two small samples of how we believe in things without needing proof. We get in elevators and airplanes with the faith that they will function properly and get us to our desired destinations safely. So it is undeniable that we all practice faith in some way or another. You may be saying to yourself, "Why do I need to believe in God to go to Heaven?" The answer to that question is you can't have one without the other. Without God, there is no Heaven and vice versa. God created Heaven, so if you don't believe in God, how can you believe in anything He created? I am talking about the fundamentals of belief. Basically, you have to believe or have faith that a place exists before you can make plans to get there. If you did not believe that place was real, you would not make the effort to get there.

I visited Japan once, and it was a wonderful experience. I'd obviously heard of Japan before, but I had not seen it in person or had any physical proof of what it was like. I had faith in my friends who organized the trip and was rewarded with a memorable experience and one of the best vacations of my life. If I had doubted my friends or not believed Japan even existed, I would have missed out on that great experience. My brother Stratton has a great saying. He would always tell me "consider the source" whenever getting information or being told something. We all know what rumors are and they can be hurtful or damaging. Who starts rumors? Unreliable sources start rumors or spread lies. Think of whom you trust in your life. Usually, the closer you are to somebody, the more you should be able to trust that person. Kids should be able to trust their parents. Friends should trust each other and most definitely, spouses should be able to trust one another. It is sad that sometimes in life even our closest relationships are unreliable and let us down. The reason for disappointments and broken trust between people is that we all have weaknesses and flaws. Sadly, the more you believe in something or someone, the more it hurts when that thing or person fails you. Fortunately, God is always trustworthy and loving. His Word—the Bible—is true and consistent throughout time, so we can know with certainty that it can be trusted and never fail us. Heaven is real, and God wants us to join Him there. God has given us the Bible as directions on how to get to Heaven. Since God is the source, we know they are true and accurate. The Bible is not just the most important written material in the history of civilization; it is the written Word of God and the only reliable source of information for us to follow that allows us to live a life honoring God and worthy of entering Heaven when our time on earth is done.

Knowing that the source (the Bible) is accurate and true, we are then responsible for following the directions accordingly to attain our desired goal. Reading the Bible or hearing scripture through Church or other Christian services is the first half of the journey. The second and most important part is following the Word or "directions." Imagine reading a map to get somewhere. If the map says go north one mile and west for half a mile but you go south for half a mile then east for one mile, you will be far from your desired destination. The map was correct, but you either did not read it correctly or did not follow its directions. When my nephew Mathew was around eight, he asked me if reading the Bible was enough to be a good Christian. I needed a way to explain to him that it was more than just reading. Mathew liked to cook at that time and thought he might want to be a chef when he grew up. I explained to him that just reading the Bible did not make someone a good Christian just as reading a cookbook did not make someone a chef. You needed to read to gain the knowledge and then go out and practice what you learned. He understood what I was telling him and that made it easier for him to grasp what he read in the Bible, was told in service, and subsequently put into practice.

We can all agree that the more you learn and the more you practice what you learn, the better you should be in that particular activity or subject. Whether you are a chef, an athlete, a singer, or a Christian, you need to constantly acquire knowledge, practice what you learn, and hone your craft. Unfortunately, doing all of this does not guarantee victory or success. Even the best of the best can lose a game or have a bad performance, just as Christians are not perfect and falter (often). Failure happens for everyone, so what is more important than success is how you react to or overcome failure. Perseverance is the key to overcoming setbacks. The big difference between worldly activities and being a Believer in Christ is the one judging us. Worldly things, such as fame, fortune, and glory are fleeting and the world judges inconsistently. Popular opinion of what is good or right varies with the times and can be as different as the people in the world. By the world's standards, today's hero could easily be tomorrow's zero. Fortunately, God is the only one who will judge us when we pass on, and we should be thankful that His ways are so much greater than ours.

Some things in life are "simple," but that does not mean that they are "easy." For instance, we all have heard the expression "don't worry, be happy," and while that sounds simple to follow, most people would agree that it is not that easy to do. So while I may make it sound simple to just have Faith and Believe in God, I will not pretend that it is an easy thing to accomplish. We live in a world that is deceived and misled by satan, and he is the biggest obstacle keeping us from living a life honoring God. That is why God sacrificed His one and only Son Jesus Christ to save our souls and give us the opportunity for redemption, which we could never attain on our own. We all need help in life. Sometimes it's a physical action (like needing a ride to get someplace or needing help moving to or from a living space), sometimes it's financial (we all know what that is like), and everyone has needed emotional help at some point in their life. Unfortunately, many people do not realize that they also need spiritual help.

I asked a friend of mine if she ever prayed, and she said, "No, I don't think I ever have." I told her that she had more than likely prayed before but just didn't realize that she was praying. I explained it like this. When her son got injured playing sports, I asked her what went through her mind. She told me she was worried and hoped he was ok. As she continued hoping ("Please be ok!"), she did not realize that she was actually praying for her son. She just didn't know who she was praying to. The main difference between praying and hoping is who you want to hear your message and who actually hears your thoughts and knows your heart and innermost feelings. Many of us have heard or said the expression "I am praying for you (or praying for something)," but what does that really mean and who are we or they praying to? When you want or ask for something, two things matter: (1) what you are asking for and (2) whom you are asking it from. A grandchild has a better chance asking for a dollar from Grandma or Grandpa than they would asking for it from a complete stranger.

As I mentioned earlier, God and Heaven are tied together and you can't have one without the other. Ironically, the question "where do YOU want to go?" is tightly related to another question. Who hears your prayers? If the answer to the first question is Heaven, then the answer to the second question should be God. These are simple facts that once accepted; we can begin learning and growing spiritually. It is not a coincidence that the Bible also teaches us how to pray. God wants to fill us with His grace and gives us every opportunity to allow Him in. Satan tries to govern this world and will do what he can to keep us from the salvation of God. When tragedy strikes or things aren't going the way we want, the temptation is to quit. Disappointments take a toll on us in many ways, and if we think there is no help coming or the situation is unbearable, we could fall to satan and lose hope. Fortunately, God never fails us, and the more we lean on Him, the less we depend on things in the world, even if we do not understand.

My grace is sufficient for you,
for My power is made perfect in weakness.
(2 Corinthians 12:9–11)

God is always present, and He is at His strongest when we are at our weakest. So often, people will pray or plead with God when they are desperate but keep Him at a distance when things are going smoothly. It is much more sincere to keep God in your heart at all times and not just when you need help. Think of your closest friends and family members. You share good and bad times alike but if you only called them when you needed help or were in trouble, I don't think they would consider you a good friend. On the flip side, if you only wanted to spend "good times" with them and were not there to support or help them during times of need, you would then be considered a "fair-weather friend" and not a true friend. Fortunately, God is there for us at all times and is much more than any friend or family member could be. He is our Lord and Savior!

It is very ironic that some nonbelievers will turn to God in desperation while some "believers" turn away from God during hardships and struggle. Fortunately, God is loving and forgiving and always wants what is best for us. I know this last statement might be hard to believe with all of the bad things that go on in this world. The writing of this chapter took place in 2020, in the middle of the COVID-19 pandemic, which has been ravaging the world and causing death and other losses in catastrophic numbers across the globe. In times like these, it is easy to lose Faith. Ironically, it is during struggle when Faith should be at its strongest. As I mentioned previously, it may sound simple but it is not easy. It would be easy to have Faith when everything is going well and life is easy for us. True Faith is when you believe in God and stay true to His Word when going through hard times. I am sure you will agree that your closest friends or people in your life are the ones who went through tough times with you; people who stuck by you or supported you if/when you were down or in a bad place. In the same way, God is always there for us, even if we don't see Him or it does not seem like it. God is everywhere at all times and knows everything about us. He knows what we do (good and bad), knows what is on our minds, and most importantly, He knows our hearts. People can fool other people, but they cannot fool God.

We are limited in our capacity to comprehend what God has planned for us, and that is why it is better to trust in Him and allow Him to work through us rather than questioning everything and trying to do things on our own. Many people think they are capable of controlling their lives and need explanations to understand everything; however, God's ways are so much higher than our way of thinking that we can't comprehend His plan for us or those in our lives. Even the smartest scientists and doctors do not have answers or explanations for everything. If they did, they would have found a cure for cancer long ago and we would not be victims of COVID-19. The sooner we realize that God is in control and allow His grace and mercy into our lives, the sooner we will be able to live with peace and harmony. The first step to having Faith and believing in God starts with accepting Jesus Christ as your Lord and Savior, confessing and repenting your sins, and allowing God into your heart. This three-part act starts your relationship with God just as inputting an address in your GPS gets you started on your trip somewhere. This may sound like a simple choice but choosing a destination for a trip is only the first step and usually the easiest. It takes much more effort and commitment to actually travel the path needed to get where you want to be.

If you have chosen Heaven as the place where you want to spend eternity after you pass from this world, you now need the directions to get you there. As I mentioned before, God wants us to join Him in Heaven and has lovingly provided His Word the Bible to give us guidance. Reading the Bible is not any easy task and learning to live a life honoring God is even more challenging. Using a GPS to reach a destination by car is easy for most of us, but imagine how difficult it would be to reach your destination if you did not know how to drive or worse, had never even seen or heard of a car! In some ways, that is what it is like for someone to just pick up a Bible, start reading it, and declare themselves a Christian. We all know the saying "crawl before you walk and walk before you run" as meaning to take your time to develop whatever it is you are trying to accomplish. Learning to accept the Lord and allowing Him to do marvelous things in your life as you read the Bible also takes time.

This aspect might be difficult for some people to grasp because for most destinations, the trip or travel time is rather short. The reality is the longer it takes to get somewhere usually means the more important the destination is. If you are just picking up lunch, you are not driving hours to get it; however, we sit in planes for hours and deal with the hassle of the airport to go on vacations or important business trips. Getting a college degree takes a certain number of years and usually the higher the degree, the longer the education process. How long have you waited, worked, or "traveled" to reach a certain position in your life? Our most valued relationships are usually the ones that we have worked on or more accurately, shared with others in our lives the longest. The longer you are willing to work on something, the more important that thing must be to you. They say patience is a virtue. Unfortunately, most of us lack that virtue. If you are one of those people, you might not like what I am about to tell you. Living a life honoring God and being worthy of entering Heaven is a journey that will take a lifetime! Imagine driving your car to reach some place and knowing it will take you the rest of your life to get there with many obstacles, distractions, and temptations constantly trying to pull you off course. No one would be able to accomplish this feat alone. Fortunately for us, we are not alone. Besides our human support, God is at our side cheering and encouraging us when we follow His guidance and forgiving us and supporting us when we stray from the course. This lifelong journey might sound too daunting but if the task is that challenging, imagine how wonderful spending eternity in Heaven must be. Nothing in this world comes close to the splendor of Heaven and when you allow God into your life, you can achieve or overcome anything, even the biggest obstacles or challenges that arise.

Japan 2004. Thank you to the Uyedas and Hagas
for a great trip and memorable experience!

His Way

While I was in college at the University of Colorado Boulder, I was returning to my dorm from early Mass; it was a beautiful Sunday morning and all that surrounded me was a fresh layer of pristine white snow on the ground, clear blue sky, and bright warm sunshine. I did not see anyone else on campus and was taken in by the peaceful silence that accompanied me. I remember that moment when I reflected on why I went to Mass every Sunday. As a youngster, I went to Mass with my Family because that's what we did, and I never questioned it. I used to ask my parents why I had to go to Sunday school when I already went to Mass and had traditional school from Monday through Friday. They explained the importance of Sunday school but to a fourth grader missing football games on TV, it did not make much sense. It all came to me that day as I walked on campus after Mass. No one forced me to attend Sunday Mass when I was in college, but I realized the value of spending personal quality time with God and church is where I was able to do that best at that time. It felt so good walking home that beautiful day, and I felt like God had given me a special gift to enjoy. I greatly appreciated that feeling and realized that I did nothing to deserve such a gift, and it was all God's doing.

My life has been filled with so much joy, and I have been told that I am "lucky"; however, I believe that it is not luck but God's grace that blesses me. My Family and Friends are the best and the love and support they give me are invaluable. I've always accepted the ups and downs and successes and failures in life with a positive attitude. I've never let the bad times or disappointments get me down, and I don't let triumphs and achievements go to my head (although you may hear otherwise from my friends). I thought I was in control of my life and could take everything in stride, including going through a divorce; however, as my Father's health declined and took a major hit in 2003, I quickly realized how little I could control in my life. Pops was my mentor, coach, strength, and buddy, and we had as close a relationship as a father and son could have. Back in August of 2003, my Pops had a stroke and was in the hospital recovering from surgery. He had been on a ventilator for two days after the surgery, and the doctor told us if he did not start breathing on his own, we might lose him. Immediately after that conversation, I ran to the hospital chapel, got on my knees, and prayed, "Please, God, take anything else from me but please don't take my Dad!" Fortunately, my Dad recovered; however, my Grandma passed away that September, and my wife left me in November. I still remember a friend telling me how bad my year was and that she hoped the New Year would be better. At first glance, it might look like a bad year, but my grandma was ninety-seven years old, living in a care home, and was patiently waiting for the Lord to take her home. One day Granny told us she saw an Angel the night before and told the Angel she was ready to go home with her. The Angel told my Grandma that she was there for the two ladies across the hall but that she would be back for my Grandma a little later. I thought Granny was just hallucinating but was amazed when I saw the two empty beds in the room across the hall and was informed that both ladies passed during the night. A short time after that day, God took my Grandma home to Heaven. As for my wife, she was not happy and no longer wanted to live in Hawaii. After our divorce, she was able to move back to the mainland and start a new life. She was happier, and I had more time to spend with family and help take care of Pops.

Turns out God knew exactly what was needed even though I had no idea at the time of my prayer. Think about this, we have all gone through ordeals or heard of tragedies and have asked, "Why God?" We can't understand why such things occur. On the other hand, we rarely feel the same way when good things happen. In fact, many nonbelievers will use this situation to question God's existence. I am sure you have heard people say, "If God is real, why does He let people suffer?" That is a very good question and just more reason we need to have Faith. It is so easy to follow or believe someone or something if they always give us what we want, but that does not make it best for us. If you are a parent, you understand what I am talking about. You want the best for your child and want to raise them correctly, but that does not mean giving them everything and anything they want. As a parent, especially of infants and young children, you should know what is best for your child and that might include discipline that the child might not like. Your child may not understand your reasoning but as they grow to love and believe in you, they will accept your ways. Having a relationship with God is a little like that. As the Bible says:

His ways are not our ways.
(Isaiah 55:8)

We cannot imagine or comprehend God's greatness; however, the more you allow Him to bless you with His grace, the more you will accept His guidance (and discipline) and not question things that happen in your life. God is always looking out for us and wants the best for us; however, we must allow Him into our hearts. Make right decisions and put forth the effort needed to accomplish the best results. Putting your faith in the Lord and allowing Him to lead you is the first step, but that does not mean sitting back and not doing anything. Reading through the Bible after my Father's passing helped me cope with my sorrow; however, God had greater plans for me. As the months passed and I let God's grace fill my heart, God allowed me to fully appreciate the love that I had for my Father and that love did not diminish with his passing. If anything, my love for my Dad grew even stronger after he passed. Pop's legacy that he left me, my family, and everyone that he touched during his life on earth was loving others and having Faith in the Lord. There was nothing that I could do to prevent the passing of my Pops, but I could do something about what I would do after that. I accepted the pain, realized my limitations, and allowed God to work through me. Acceptance over understanding is an example of Faith and one of the first steps in trusting the Lord's way. The sooner we realize that fact the better because the basic truth is we have little to no control over what goes on in this world. So much happens in this world that does not make sense to us. We might think life is unfair and that some people get all the breaks. Fortunately for us, God loves everyone the same, for Scripture says:

> For there is no respect of persons with God.
> (Romans 2:11)

This Scripture means that God does not show favoritism. He loves everyone the same, regardless of age, race, wealth (or lack thereof), looks, or any other attribute the world uses to judge us. This may be a hard concept to grasp as we see so many people in this world "get away" with things while good and innocent people suffer; however, in our limited capacity to understand God's ways, we do not know the whole story. Many "successful" people of the world may, in fact, be suffering internally while others we think are less fortunate could be developing perseverance that gives them strength and comfort. One thing we do know is that when it comes to suffering in the form of natural disasters or health issues, no one is immune or "above it." When a hurricane or earthquake hits, it takes down everything and anything in its path; similarly, COVID-19 has taken too many lives and has negatively affected the entire civilized world. It does not matter if you are rich and famous or poor and unknown, this virus is a threat to all of us the same. In a positive way, God judges everyone equally based on His laws and Word. There is no "buying your way out" or "taking short cuts" when it comes to honoring Jesus Christ as your Lord and Savior. You do not have to be rich or successful according to the world to be a "good and faithful servant" to the Lord. In fact, the Bible warns that it is harder for a rich person to enter Heaven because of the temptation to worship their worldly wealth. Please do not be mistaken; God has nothing against wealth and success; in fact, He *wants* us to prosper. There are many Scriptures in the Bible where God displays or tells us His good intentions for us, such as:

> For I know the plans I have for you,
> plans to prosper you and not harm your,
> plans to give you hope and a future.
> (Jeremiah 29:11)

God is happy when we find success or flourish in life. Wealth does not and should not define a person, and God definitely looks past a person's financial status on Judgement Day. Just because someone is wealthy does not mean they cannot be a good Christian; however, if someone lives a life focused on attaining wealth and neglects the more important things, then money becomes their "God" and that is what the Bible warns against. Most of us have heard the saying "money is the root of all evil"; however, money is not the problem, it is people's love (or more accurately lust) for money that causes trouble. The correct Bible verse is this:

> For the love of money is the root of all evil.
> (1 Timothy 6:10)

God knows everything that goes on and because He loves all of us the same and judges everyone fairly, we can be secure in our lives and trust in His ways, regardless of our "worldly status." The main thing to understand, or better yet accept, is the fact that God is in control and not us. Take a moment to reflect on times in your life, good or bad, when you could not comprehend why that event occurred, or possibly is occurring. Many times, we go through challenges in life that leave us feeling helpless or not in control of the situation, yet we somehow make it through. Take this senseless pandemic that we are currently dealing with. There are so many more questions than answers regarding the virus and its devastating effects. No one knows when or how it will end, but if you have Faith in God, then you know that He is in control and that makes it much easier to accept, even if we do not understand. Almost everything you do in life is based on what your "beliefs" are. Following directions as simple as "wear a face mask" is so easy, yet too many people don't do it because they do not "believe" it is necessary. If we are forced, either by law or by some other reason, then people will usually do what they are told. It is so much better when you do what is right because you *want* to do it rather than *have* to do it. Similarly, you must choose to receive Christ and follow God if you are truly going to have faith. No one can be forced to have faith.

You may be telling yourself, "If God is in control, then He must be responsible for all of the bad stuff that goes on in this world." On the contrary, while God *is* in control and blesses us constantly, He never curses us. This fact is so important that I will repeat it boldly: *God never curses us!* He gives us choices and allows us to make our own decisions, and if those decisions lead to destruction, we cannot blame God. We shouldn't blame anyone because blame is never part of the solution. In fact, blame could prolong the problem as it prevents us from taking responsibility for our mistakes and hinders improvement in judgement.

Think of someone you may know who never thinks they are at fault and always blames others for a bad situation. That person has probably been that way for most of their lives and won't change or improve until they have a change of heart. Blaming is a form of complaining, and complaining never solves any problem. So remember, when it comes to life and especially God, don't *B-lame*! Taking responsibility for our mistakes or finding the cause or source of something bad is not the same as blaming someone. In fact, it is the first step to making things better. We have all heard of satan, and most of us are familiar with the story of Adam and Eve and how satan, in the form of a serpent, deceived Eve into eating fruit from the Tree of Knowledge. That was humankind's first sin, and satan has been trying to get humans to sin ever since. Satan runs around our earthly world, and his strongest weapon is the same now as it was in the Garden of Eden—deception. You might be thinking there is no such thing as the devil or satan and that is exactly what Lucifer (another name satan goes by) wants you to believe. If you are not aware or do not believe there is peril, you are more likely to be careless and fall into harm's way.

Growing up in Hawaii, we are taught to respect the ocean and be careful whenever we are around it; however, too many people (locals and tourists) are not aware of or ignore the dangers and pay a dear price. Satan counts on similar ignorance and apathy to lead too many people to destruction. Adam and Eve realized their mistake and made amends by taking responsibility for their actions and not falling into the same trap. Accepting the Lord and coming to Christ makes you aware of satan and his devious ways.

Let me take this point a step further. Whatever happens to people in this world does not necessarily define them. What they do or how they react after what has happened to them (good or bad) is what really matters. Someone could win the lottery and we might think how lucky they are; however, if they waste their winnings on drugs and end up overdosing, we might not think they were winners after all. On the other hand, I have friends and family members who were struck with adversity (health or otherwise) and I marvel at their strength and perseverance to overcome the hardships they have had to endure. Two very important things occur to defeat adversities in our life: (1) is our own decision to accept the challenge facing us and to have determination to do what it takes to succeed (basically, to have perseverance) and (2) is to have support. Support comes in many forms (physical, emotional, financial, and so on) and from different sources. If something bad has happened, we need to properly assess the situation, determine how we will fix or improve it, and find the proper help or support to succeed. Fortunately, God provides comfort and support beyond our comprehension. He is always there for us, and He always knows what is best for us. If you have Faith and are able to accept His grace and guidance, you will be able to persevere through hard times. It is too bad that many of us think we know what is best for us and ignore God's signs. It is this pride that leads to further pain. If someone is not willing to listen to good advice from people who care for them, it will be much harder for them to accept guidance from God, who they cannot see or hear, and that is where Faith comes in again.

Even Christians may sometimes doubt God's presence when tragedy strikes. That is human nature. If or when doubt creeps into your heart, kick it out of there and embrace your opportunity to triumph! A setback or loss we encounter in life is actually a chance to overcome that adversity and claim victory in your life. Think how great it would be if you embraced hardships when they occurred and took the opportunity to turn them into gain. One of the many blessings that come with having Faith in the Lord is *hope*!

We also rejoice in our sufferings, because we know that suffering produces perseverance, perseverance, character; and character, hope. And hope does not disappoint us.
(Romans 5:3–5)

Everyone in this world has or will hope for something during their life. It could be something minor, such as hoping to find a parking stall at the mall close to the entry, or something huge like hoping medical test results comes back negative. Regardless of the topic, whenever we "hope" for something, that usually means the outcome is not in our control. We might not have the final say, but many times what we do in preparation can have an impact on the outcome. Going to the mall early could improve your chances for a good parking stall. A good diet along with consistent exercise could improve your health.

We have all heard the saying "that which does not kill you makes you stronger." This saying means that any adversity that we survive (physically or otherwise) should make us better or "stronger" in the future. As I mentioned previously, my Pops had a stroke in 2003, and thankfully, it did not kill him, so we were able to learn about his ailments and enjoy seven more years together before God called him home. Hardships come in all forms, but the more you overcome, the better you are equipped to deal with the next incident. If someone loses a job for the first time, it might seem devastating; however, if that person figures out why they were let go, correct the situation, and get another job, they might do better at the next job or even find a better job. Additionally, if they were to be let go again (through no fault of their own), they should be able handle the termination better than the first time they lost their job. Sometimes we have no control over what is happening in our world; however, God is always in control, therefore we do not have to add stress to stressful situations.

Those who trust in the Lord will tell you that having Faith allows you to focus on the solution rather than dwell on the problem. Think of all the things going on in your world and what control you have over them. Whether you are a Believer or not (yet), things go on in life that affect all of us similarly, yet we react in much different ways. Take COVID-19 as an example. The current pandemic has affected everyone at the same time and regulations have been placed on all of us for the welfare of society. Most of us follow the orders of wearing a mask and practice social distancing. Some take it a step further and rarely go into the public, and then there are people who do not follow any of the rules by not wearing masks and getting together for social gatherings. We may judge others but there is not much we can do about it so we trust (or blame) the system in place. Trusting those in control alleviates a lot of pressure while fighting it creates turmoil. Think of this example: When we get on a plane to fly somewhere, we put our trust in the pilot(s) to fly the plane correctly and also trust that the plane is in proper operating condition. If you thought the pilot was incompetent or the plane was faulty, would you even get on board? Having Faith and trust in God is a little like that, except pilots and mechanics are human and sometimes make mistakes or errors. God is infallible; He is always good, always just, and always loving, even if we do not see it or cannot understand it. Accepting His ways and allowing Him to guide you and persevering whenever struggles come your way are the fundamentals of Faith.

Please do not mistake acceptance with apathy. Letting God into your heart and accepting His ways does not mean doing nothing when hardships come and just blaming God. Saying, "Oh well, God must have wanted it this way," and doing nothing to improve a situation is not having Faith but laziness and a lack of courage to have the fortitude to heed His direction and persevere. Like I mentioned previously, what happens to you does not define your character. It is how you react to what happens to you that defines your character. I learned this fact when my Father went home to Heaven. Pops was a super awesome Dad, but if all I did was sulk or be sad after he passed, how would that honor him or show what kind of son he raised? In fact, that would be a travesty to the kind of Dad he was. I admitted to God that I was lost and needed His guidance more than ever. Through all of this soul searching, I feel that my relationship with God has improved tremendously and reading every day has given me personal spiritual growth. God blessed me with the knowledge that showing others love and joy in a selfless manner is the best way to express God's love. I am a better person by expressing God's love for others rather than grieving internally over my own loss. This realization gave me the opportunity to shift my focus from my own pain to helping others get through their ordeals. Caring about others rather than focusing on myself has eased my pain tremendously and given me joy knowing that my actions honor Pops and how he raised me. God's way is always best, and His ways are so much higher than we can fathom that we have to have Faith and let Him guide us and give us the energy, discipline, and determination to carry out His plans for us.

You might be wondering how you know if and when God is guiding you. God is omnipresent, omniscient, and omnipotent, meaning He is everywhere at all times and is all knowing. Even if you do not believe in God, He is still there looking over you, you are just ignoring His presence. Just because we cannot see something or choose to disregard it does not mean it does not exist or is not present. Everyone makes choices every day, and I am sure at times there have been some very difficult choices. Sometimes the most important decisions we have to make are moral decisions, especially if we think no one is watching or knows what we are doing. You might have seen a movie or show where the character has an angel on one shoulder and a devil on the other. They are both trying to persuade the character to do something good or bad. Usually this scene is used in comedy; however, in real life, this spiritual battle is very serious. When you choose to do good over evil, people will refer to "that little voice in your head," or your conscience, that tells you what to do. In reality, that is God intervening and giving you guidance. On the flip side, if you choose the wrong path and pick evil over good, you have rejected God and allowed satan to influence you. Fortunately, God is a merciful God and never gives up on us, so when we falter or make wrong decisions, God will forgive us of our sins as long as we confess and repent of them.

Because of the Lord's great love we are not consumed,
for His compassions never fail.
(Lamentations 3:22)

The good news is that the more you learn about and welcome Jesus into your heart, the more He will guide you and make it easier to make good and sound decisions. The Bible tells us that God loves us so much that he sacrificed His one and only Son Jesus Christ so that our sins could be forgiven and we could be allowed to join Him in Heaven. God was willing to do that for us so whatever goes on in this world cannot deter His love for us, and when you have a relationship with the Lord, you will be able to accept His way and gain wisdom rather than question or try to "understand" it. Along with wisdom comes peace of mind and the will to improve situations instead of complaining about them. God is always in control and it is so much better to accept, or better yet follow His ways rather than question or fight it.

I took the following picture above Makapu'u on the eastern coastline of Oahu. The picture is small since I took a panoramic shot so it does not show the true magnificence of that scene. From the majestic mountains to the deep blue ocean and up to the glorious sky filled with bright sunshine and wondrous clouds, God's artistry was on full display when I took this picture. Humans could never create such splendor, yet God's most precious creation in all of this beauty is the small black image toward the bottom left of the picture. That figure is my Mom standing on the lookout. I took this picture for her because she is an artist and wanted to paint this scene. As impressive and awesome as this view is, it pales in comparison to the gift of life and love that my Mom has given me along with all of the wonderful things God has blessed my family and me with through my Mom. I wanted to share this picture with you to emphasize that God is our great Creator and always in control, yet He cares for each and every one of us as His own precious children.

The splendor of Makapu'u. Thank you, God,
for the view and my Mom!

Your Words

Accepting the Lord and acknowledging His presence and grace for you is a wonderful thing; however, that is just the beginning of the relationship God wants to have with us. Realizing that God is in control allows you to accept events and situations, but you must also put forth action to improve and win each and every day. We have all heard the expression "he can talk the talk, but can he walk the walk?" meaning you can say you will do something, but will you actually do it? The important thing to remember is that *both* the words and the action are important. If you say, "I am a loser and do not want to work anymore," then go out and get fired, you talked the talk and walked the walk, but that does not make it a good thing. God hears everything, even our innermost thoughts, so it is very important to not only speak with wisdom and kindness but to also have good and pure thoughts. I remember as a kid we used to say, "Sticks and stones may break my bones but words will never hurt me." Words might not hurt you physically but they can sure damage you in other aspects. Lies or rumors could cost you a job or your reputation, and angry words have damaged or ended many relationships. These are just a few examples of how our words can be very destructive. Fortunately, our words can also encourage, cheer, educate, and have many other positive influences in our lives. I hope this book is a good example.

I previously told you that God is in control and that His ways are best to accept and follow; however, that does not mean we do not have any impact on how we live our lives. God constantly gives us opportunities in the form of choices and decisions, so we cannot blame Him if we make poor choices. God is present through the good times and bad, whether we acknowledge Him or not. I am sure you have seen or heard athletes or entertainers "thank the Lord" for winning a trophy or award, but how much more powerful would it be to thank Him even in defeat? God does not have a "favorite team" and He does not root for a particular player or person. We should all thank Him for the opportunity to even play the game, much less winning it. More often, the outcome of an event is based on choices and decisions the participants made before and during the event, like training, game plans, and so on. God is our final judge, and He is in control of the universe; however, He gives us choices to make and does not weigh every decision the same. What shirt you choose to wear to work probably is of little or no importance to God but choosing to tell the truth or lie about something has much heavier consequences. We like to think we can control what goes on in our lives, and for a few small things, we can. One of the most important things we control is our *words*. We are all affected by what we say and how we say it and in return, respond to how we are spoken to. Kind and encouraging words can make someone's day, but negative or hurtful words cause strife. How you speak and what you speak are so important and reflect the type of person you are. We all react to the type of conversations that we are exposed to. If you have a coworker who is always complaining or a boss who speaks angrily or disrespectfully, how do you view that person? It is much better to be around people who speak in a positive manner, so take a moment to reflect on how you speak to people in your life. The Bible is very clear about how important our words are with over thirty scriptures that give guidance. Most of these scriptures come from the Book of Proverbs, which gives wisdom to lead a Holy, prosperous, peaceful, and fulfilling life.

The words of the reckless pierce like swords,
but the tongue of the wise brings healing.
(Proverbs 12:18)

How people talk to one another often depends on who they are talking to and the situation. A coach trying to teach a team or a boss correcting an employee will talk much differently than a child talking to their parent or a couple having a romantic conversation. Communication is more successful when proper words are combined with the right attitude. Respect should be constant, regardless of the situation. In a disagreement or an argument, if you speak respectfully, you have a much better chance at resolving the issue. Words carry so much weight, not just in conversation but also in how we choose to live. Words usually precede action and sometimes even dictate action. You know the saying "if you say you can or say you can't, you are correct," meaning if you think and say you can or will do something, then you will find a way to do it, but if you don't think you can do something, then you probably won't. This saying basically means your words often precede your actions, which is why you should choose your words wisely. Another take on this quote is that if you want to do something, you will find a way to do it, but if you do not want to do something, you will find an excuse not to do it. I am sure you know people you consider positive and those you consider negative. I am guessing that the positive people achieve more and complain less than the negative people. I am not generalizing or defining people. It can come down to specific situations. I consider myself to be a positive person who most times says or thinks, "I can do this." Yet there are areas of my life where I might not be so sure, or more accurately, enthusiastic about doing something. If you've seen my messy house or office, you know cleaning up clutter is not one of my motivations! We should do what we say and say what we mean and most of all, try to keep it positive. Saying I am going to steal something and then doing it does not make you honest, it makes you a fool. Keeping your word is a sign of integrity and generates trust between people, but our words should be constructive not destructive. God's words give guidance, encouragement, caution, and wisdom. His words, found in the Bible, can be trusted at all times and in all circumstances because He is always true, and His love for us never wavers.

Since our words are so important, we need to learn how to use them properly. I am not talking grammatically, although that is essential too; I am referring to how we communicate, or more importantly, how we connect with others. Our words should also be used to encourage or enhance our own lives. With your words declaring that Heaven is where you want to go after passing on from this world, you have taken the first step to improving your life right now. Every journey begins with the first step, and the more steps you take, the further you will travel, unless you are walking in a circle! Direction and pace often influence your travel success, and the same is true of your words. Little steps are easier to take than large leaps, and humble confidence is much better than boastful assertions. Declaring you want to go to Heaven is a great statement. No one should consider it boastful or egotistical. On the contrary, claiming your desire to join God for eternity also means admitting your shortcomings and willingness to work on a daily basis to live a life worthy of entering Heaven. In fact, choosing to spend eternity in Heaven and trusting God as your Lord and Savior is one of the more humbling statements you can make and one that requires much commitment.

In this world, people claim many things under all types of circumstances. It may be a small physical achievement ("I will lose ten pounds by a certain date"), it might be a financial statement ("I will save $100 a month"), or it could be an emotional or moral act ("I will stop treating my employees poorly"). This line of thought is the same as setting goals for one's self, and like goals, the bigger they are, the longer or more effort it usually takes to complete them. For instance, if your goal was to save enough money to buy a nice car, it would most likely take longer and more effort (sacrifices to save money) than if your goal was to buy a simple skateboard. Someone who wants to become a doctor will have to go through much more education and training than someone who just wants a high school diploma. I am not saying one is better or more important than the other; I am simply making the point that the "bigger" or more important a goal is to someone, the more that person is willing to take more time, put more effort, and make more sacrifices to achieve their goal. In this world, people judge each other based on their own point of view, which can lead to inconsistency and misunderstanding. I am sure you have heard the saying "one man's trash is another man's treasure." This saying not only pertains to physical items but also to philosophical issues. These differences of opinions vary in degree of intensity from insignificant to the cause of wars and bloodshed. As I am writing this, the 2022 US presidential election has just concluded, and even within our own country, there are strong differences in how people think the government should be run. Conflict often arises through lack of agreement or unity and is a main cause of unrest on a macro and microscale. Countries in conflict with each other go to war similar to a couple in conflict, just on different scales. Agreement deters conflict between parties involved, and in most cases, an agreement is reached when both sides see the same thing, even if it is from different points of view. A good example of this is the sun. Everyone agrees that the sun is bright and hot, regardless of where you live on this planet (even though some might say it is hotter in some places). Certain physical laws are undeniable. My focus is on the spiritual laws.

One thing that this world has a common acknowledgement of is money. Money is a very important tool that most societies value and try to accumulate. I use the term tool because, like a tool, money can help you build or accomplish good things; however, if used incorrectly or inappropriately, it can harm or even destroy you. Although most people agree that money is a necessity, the level of importance, or how we value that money, varies greatly. Also, money is something that has what I call "subjective objectivity," meaning an objective number is looked at subjectively. Let me give you an example: If a three-bedroom, two-bathroom house costs $500,000.00, would that be expensive or cheap? In Hawaii, most people would consider that cheap; however, in other states, they might say that is expensive. The amount is the same and objective, but the view of it is subjective depending on your location and/or situation. Here is another example: Is a millionaire rich? To most of us, they are, but to a billionaire, maybe not. So many things in this world depend on your perspective, circumstances, or what other people think. However, when you choose God as your Lord and Savior and want to go to Heaven, He becomes the only judge that matters. There will still be issues to deal with and having God in your life does not guarantee an easy lifestyle, but it does assure you that He is by your side and has your back at all times. God's promise to His people gives you the confidence to live without fear.

So do not fear, for I am with you;
do not be dismayed, for I am your God.
I will strengthen you and help you;
I will uphold you with my righteous right hand.
(Isaiah 41:10)

Since God has given us His spoken words through the Bible, we have the perfect source to give us guidance and direction. Your words proclaim your actions and affect others in many ways so choose and use them wisely to achieve great things and bring the glory of Jesus Christ to others. As I mentioned previously, part of accepting Jesus Christ as your Lord and Savior is confessing and repenting of your sins. Confessing generally means admitting your sins or wrongdoings, and the dictionary defines repent as expressing sincere regret or remorse about one's wrongdoings or sin; however, the Biblical meaning for repent takes it even further. To repent of our sins means to turn away from and change our ways. When we sin, we not only need to confess our sins but we need to try our best not to repeat that mistake. If someone is caught shoplifting and confesses to the store owner and gives back the stolen item, the owner might forgive him and not prosecute. However, if the same person comes back the very next day and is caught shoplifting again, that person has not truly repented and chances are the owner will prosecute the second time around. Maybe the criminal has an illness and can't help shoplifting but as humans, we can't always judge perfectly, and our emotions often cloud our judgement. Fortunately, God has true clarity in His judgement, and He knows not just what we say and do (even in private), He knows our hearts and intentions.

Judgement Day will come to everyone, whether you believe in God or not. The good news is that while we are here on earth, we can make a positive impact with our words and actions. I once heard a sports commentator describe NFL pre-season football games like this: "They don't count, but they do matter," and that was a very appropriate description, meaning the win-loss records do not affect the regular season but how players perform or if they get injured does have a direct effect on the upcoming season. Similarly, our words may or may not count toward much, especially if we are talking to ourselves, but they do matter to those who are affected by them. Little victories or progress can add up to prominent success and many times it starts with "I can" or "I will" (add something positive) or "I won't" (add something negative). The saying "a smile can light up a room" is similar to what the Bible says.

> A cheerful look brings joy to the heart,
> and good news gives health to the bones.
> (Proverbs 15:30)

The Scripture above describes two things we exhibit: (1) our attitude and (2) our words, which have a great effect on those around us. If you are cheerful and go through life smiling and using kind words, people will enjoy your company and listen more intently when you speak. On the other hand, people who are unpleasant or speak negatively all the time are most likely avoided. The difference can be as simple as the words each person chooses, not just in communication but also in how they perceive or treat their own everyday activities. Let's use work as an example. It does not matter what the job or career is, when you wake up in the morning, you can say, "I *have* to go to work," or you can say, "I *get* to go to work." The event is the same but the perspective is different, and that can make a big difference. Activities and events we like or enjoy are described as things we *get* to do, while things we *have* to do are usually not by choice; however, if it is a task or responsibility such as going to work or picking up the kids, you can still take a positive approach. The more things you do or say in a positive manner might not lessen the burdens you encounter in life, but it will affect how you endure or overcome those trials, and God is the biggest influence in helping you persevere. It takes time to develop a positive (or negative) outlook on life, and we are dependent on so many things. The world is inconsistent and unstable when it comes to moral foundations, and that is why God is vital in our spiritual warfare. He is the one true and trustworthy source who never wavers and never fails. I said previously to take small steps first and if accepting the Lord into your heart is too big a step right now, that is ok because God is not leaving, and He will not abandon you.

You can start by asking God to show you His ways. By just asking Him to show you His love or be part of your life, you can benefit greatly, but you have to be willing to participate in the wonders ahead. Let's take a simple task to start. Think of an issue you have. It could be a physical, financial, emotional, or other type of situation you are dealing with. Start telling yourself you *get* to take care of that issue rather than *have* to (like the example of going to work). After speaking the words, act on them. If your job has you down, think of positive aspects. The mere fact that you have a job is positive, especially in these unstable times. Breaking down issues into simpler, smaller tasks makes it easier to complete your goals and prevents you from getting overwhelmed. Only God can do everything all at once, so when you find yourself needing help, ask Him, and He will deliver. You may not agree with or comprehend His ways but God knows what is best for us even when we do not. Give yourself little exercises or challenges on being a positive influence, and you will see the good that it can do. Tell yourself something like "I will help someone today" or "I will cut out swearing" and then make good on your words. Keep stacking positive actions, and not only will you feel better but people in your life will too.

Most things in life take time to develop or complete. As I have mentioned before, the more important the subject or result is, the longer it should take to accomplish; however, we also need to appreciate the little things in life as we progress through the long hauls. That is why I encourage you to take each day as a challenge or event and within each day, take care of whatever you can to win the day. As I write this paragraph, it is 4:30 p.m. on Saturday, November 28, 2020. This is a general recap of my day.

7:30 a.m. I pick up food for lunch, then go to the store to return two short extension cords and buy a longer extension cord so I can use my new clippers to cut my hair.

8:30 a.m. I take car to Auto Shop for an oil change and new tires. My sister Rella picks me up and takes me home to use Mom's car until my car is ready.

9:15 a.m. I meet with my clients to discuss their renovation project.

10:30 a.m. I meet Mom and Rella at a restaurant to get a snack.

11:00 a.m. I go to the bank to pay a bill.

11:30 a.m. I go home and put in a load of laundry.

Noon. I go to my friends' house while laundry is washing to pick up some avocados that they picked for me from their tree.

1:30 p.m. Back home, I put the laundry in the dryer. While my clothes are drying, I give myself a haircut (pandemic safety), vacuum off the loose hair, then take a shower.

3:00 p.m. I write a check for my insurance bill and prepare to mail it.

3:30 p.m. Rella takes me to pick up car from Auto Shop. I pick her up after she drops off the extra car at home and mail my insurance payment on the way back to my home.

4:00 p.m. Back at home, I take my clothes from the dryer and fold them. After folding my clothes, I sit down to write.

4:30 p.m. I am writing this section while eating my late lunch!

I accomplished all of the things that I had planned to do and, in my opinion, "won the day." Each task or errand was simple but getting all of them done and still having time to write is a small victory in my book (this book I guess). It all started when I woke up in the morning and asked God to watch over me and guide me through the day to accomplish what I needed to do, not from my perspective but for His purpose. It has been a very productive day, and it was a combination of my words and His way that worked out beautifully. The focus is not on the tasks but on the positive influence that God has in our lives. If you are a believer in Jesus Christ, I should not have to convince you of this revelation; however, if you are not a believer (yet) or feel skeptical of His marvelous plans for you, just give yourself the opportunity to be blessed by God's grace and mercy. You will be astonished by what you are able to accomplish and truly grateful for the wonders that God will perform.

Let your words set a path for you and use your words to help others as well. Follow your words with action and stay true and positive. Ask God for help and guidance, and thank Him for His blessings. Most importantly, choose and use your words wisely because your words are powerful!

Mom's winning and positive words always come through
(even if her mask does not cover her nose during COVID-19)!

The Silver Fox

Today was like every other day
Flowers bloomed, others died,
Children laughed while others cried.

Yes, today was like every other day
Because I thought of you
And missed you dearly!

I wrote the poem above when I was in college, and at the time, I did not know whom I wrote it for or why it even came to me. After my Pops passed away in 2010, I knew exactly what that poem meant and whom it was for.

My Father, Lawrence Y.F. Pang, grew up in a large family with three brothers and five sisters. His parents immigrated to Hawaii from China, so as a child, he was not raised in a Christian household. God had a special plan for my Dad, and after he was baptized, he graduated from Saint Louis Catholic High School. After attending and graduating from Colorado State University, Pops returned to Hawaii and married my Mom, Luella L. Pang. Mom was raised as a Catholic Christian and graduated high school from Sacred Hearts Academy followed by Mount Saint Mary's Catholic University. Mom and Pops were devout Catholic Christians and did their best to raise their three kids that way. This chapter is not a biography about my Dad; however, I do want to tell you a little bit about his background. What is more important than objective facts about his life is sharing the strong faith that he had in the Lord and how God blessed my Dad throughout the years. My Dad's relationship with the Lord was very private and personal. Pops was very devoted to God, but he was not boastful about it. He never acted privileged or "special" because of his relationship with God, and Pops never put himself above others because of his Faith and beliefs or because of others' differences. My Dad was known by many names, Lawrence, Larry, Ah Fong, Mr. Pang, Silver Fox, Dad, Pops, and Grandpa depending on your relationship with him. No matter how you addressed him, you did so with love and respect because that is how he treated you. Pops had a great sense of humor and such a joyful attitude.

He loved to make others laugh with jokes and fun stories and though he may not have seemed humble when socializing and bantering with friends and family, often proclaiming his "good looks," deep down, he was truly humble. Humility can be shown in different ways and is one of the valuable traits that God wants us to have in ourselves and endear to others.

After my Father retired, he would walk every morning to get exercise. He would walk from our house, pass the shopping mall, then turn around and come back. On the return trip, he would stop at our Church and go inside for a few minutes. He told me it was a good place to "cool off" after the walk, but I know it was much more meaningful than that. I know my Dad had deep inner conviction in the Lord and that is one of the reasons God blessed him with the strength and spirit to persevere through all of his afflictions. I am certain that God's blessing and grace bestowed upon Pops started long before I was born and enabled him to be such a great father. My Pops provided everything I can think of for a nourishing and enjoyable childhood. He and my Mom were not perfect, but they were the most loving and supportive parents anyone could have. Throughout middle and high school (long before smart phones and Instagram), Pops would take time off from work to help with school events that I was involved with. From barbecuing for us at a class picnic to taking pictures at our May Day festival and Senior Day, Pops sacrificed his time to make sure his son and his friends enjoyed the most from that day or event. When it came to sports, my Dad was always there to record the event. Sometimes he would take pictures of my friends playing in games that I wasn't even participating! For my Dad, it was always about giving to others.

Do you remember the Mountain Dew catchphrase "good old Mountain Dew!"? It was the slogan for the soda when it first came out in the 1970's. That slogan will always remind me of Pops. We were on a family summer trip and were driving on a single lane highway, which was log jammed for some reason. It was a very hot summer day and not all of the cars back then had air conditioning (or power windows). We were at a standstill, and the car in front of us was a station wagon with kids in the back. They were suffering in the summer heat. We had a cooler full of cold drinks, so my Dad got out of our car and offered the car in front of us some "good old Mountain Dew!" The parents were very grateful, and the kids enjoyed the refreshing beverage. Being a little kid of six or seven, I did not understand why my Dad gave our soda to strangers. When I asked him why he did that, he told me that it is important to help others when you can, even if you do not know them. I will always remember that generous gesture from my Pops, but more importantly, the lesson he taught me about generosity and caring for others. As an adult striving to improve my relationship with God, I realize God's Holy Spirit was working through my Dad that day as well as the many other times he gave of himself for the benefit of others. If you are familiar with the Bible, or if you are not, giving of one's self for others is the number one message being proclaimed and the greatest gift from Jesus Christ as our Lord and Savior.

Just as the Son of Man did not come to be served, but to serve, and to give His life as a ransom for many.
(Mathew 20:28)

Another big thing that Pops instilled in me was that if you decide to do something, try your best and give it your best effort. That way, if you succeed, you will have earned the rewards but if you do not succeed, you can be proud of your effort and not be ashamed of anything. Not succeeding in something or not getting the outcome you desired is not the same as failure. Most times, we learn more from our mistakes or "failures" than we do from our victories or successes. The key is to learn and not give up. Jesus knows we are not perfect and loves us even more because of our shortcomings. My Dad knew I had many flaws, and as parents, he and my Mom did their best to teach and guide me. I may not have understood or even agreed with their actions at the time but I trusted that they had my best interest in making their decisions. Similarly, God loves us as His children, and we need to trust His guidance, especially when we do not understand. That is what Faith is all about. Ironically, when we do not get our way or do not agree with a decision levied upon us, it is much easier to accept authority and follow directions or consequences than to oppose and fight it. Whether it is a parent teaching a child, a coach coaching a team, or a boss guiding an employee, if we receive and follow the instruction with a positive attitude, we avoid conflict and attain rewards much easier. When we follow directions or guidance from authority, it alleviates pressure on us, which should bring peace of mind and eliminate stress. If a boss tells the employee to do a certain task and the employee follows the directions perfectly, there is no pressure on the employee for the outcome of that task since the responsibility falls on the boss. As such, when we listen to and obey God's Word, we receive enduring peace and rid ourselves of stress, knowing that God is in control and has our best interest in mind. On the other hand, when you ignore or protest against authority, conflict and struggles occur. You also take on an added burden when you decide to do things "your way." We recently voted in a new mayor where I live and along with him, we have a new regime of directors. Each director has good intentions for how they want their department to succeed, so they are implementing their operational procedures. Not everyone agrees with the new direction; however, it is our responsibility as civil servants to follow accordingly.

My Father worked for a large company and was a loyal employee for many years. I asked him once if he wanted to get promoted and be like one of his bosses. He had a very profound response that I will always remember. He told me it was better to be called a peasant and treated like a king than called a king and treated like a peasant. He told me that titles were not as important as how you treated people or were treated by others. When I asked him about the money he could make, he reminded me that money was not the most important thing when considering a job or career. I might not have understood much then as a teenager, but as an adult, I understand what he meant. Had Pops pushed for a promotion, he might have gotten more money; however, his new position may have caused more stress or not allowed him the freedom to spend time with me at the events mentioned previously. His perspective was spot on and supported by the following Scripture:

Better to be a nobody and yet have a servant
than pretend to be somebody and have no food.
(Proverbs 12:9)

The scripture above describes the way Pop's went about his life when it came to accolades and titles. The only time he used names or titles was to acknowledge friends or family or to describe people in personal settings. My dad and our family liked to give each other nicknames as terms of endearment. Having a full head of silky silver hair and being witty and humorous, Silver Fox was the natural moniker for my Father, and he was proud of that nickname because it was given to him out of love and respect. One word that truly exemplified Pops was *joyful*. People often think that joy and happiness mean the same thing; however, while both are good, they have significant differences. I learned the difference from Pastor Wayne Cordero, and I was fortunate to meet him and thank him for his words of wisdom. Pastor Wayne described the difference like this: *Happiness* is what we feel when good things happen *to* us, while *joy* is what we have inside—it comes *from* us so that we can share it with others. We basically feel happiness when we receive something positive, and we give our joy to others to create happiness for them. I think this description is spot on, and Pastor Wayne went further in his instruction as he informed us how we lose our joy, and that is by *complaining*! I am in absolute agreement with the belief that we lose joy by complaining. If you have ever seen or heard someone complain, I am sure you would not describe that person as joyful!

With God in his life, the Silver Fox handled most situations with the right attitude. I cannot say Pops never complained, but I can say that he *rarely* complained, and in those brief moments, it was more a reaction to something sudden and unexpected than an ongoing long-term situation. My Dad dealt with many health issues, starting with diabetes until his passing from congestive heart failure. He endured many physical trials that included insulin shots every day, several surgeries, dialysis, and about a dozen trips to the emergency room. During the summer of 2007, we went to watch my nephew compete in the World Taekwondo Championships in Arkansas. We had just returned to my brother's home in Las Vegas and were heading out to dinner when Pops said he felt weak and almost collapsed. Turns out Pops contracted some sort of virus in Arkansas that affected his heart, and he ended up having emergency heart surgery to implant a pacemaker with a defibrillator. The hospital discharged him the day after surgery, which we protested, and he had complications that night and had to be rushed back to the ER. To make matters worse, his kidneys were failing, which we knew about, so he had to start dialysis during that same ordeal. We ended up staying in Vegas for thirty days until he was healthy enough to travel back home to Honolulu.

The most amazing thing that I remember about that entire drama was that my Dad never once complained, not about his physical pain and discomfort or the hassle of going in and out of the hospital or the burden of going to dialysis. In fact, he apologized to me and the rest of my family for being a burden. What an awesome dude; he is going through all of these physical and psychological trials and he is more concerned about his family missing work! Not only did Pops not complain about the situation, but he spread joy to those around him with his jovial personality and exuberant positive attitude. The thirty days were spent as an extended family vacation rather than a tiresome ordeal.

My Dad's physical trauma in the summer of 2007 was the start of his earthly body breaking down. Ironically, but not surprisingly, his spiritual strength grew as his physical health declined. Pops always had inner strength and peace of mind knowing exactly whom he was and what he needed to do in whatever role God asked of hm. As he aged and was no longer able to do the physical things of his youth, Pops gained wisdom and spiritual knowledge that he was grateful to receive and willing to share. The Silver Fox spent countless hours in prayer, whether he was at dialysis, some doctor appointment, or just relaxing at home. God gave him peace and strength to persevere through all of his trials and tribulations with a smile on his face and a friendly demeanor for those he encountered. Pops had a great sense of humor, and one of his favorite lines was when a doctor asked him, "Mr. Pang, how do you feel?" Pops would reply, "With my hands."

Pops knew the importance of staying positive and sharing optimism with others, and the following scripture describes my dad's attitude quite accurately:

> A cheerful heart is good medicine,
> but a crushed spirit dries up the bones.
> (Proverbs 17:22)

Pops definitely had a cheerful heart and everyone who knew him would attest to that. What my Dad accomplished from an "earthly" view may seem modest, and that is fine because he was a modest and humble man; however, the impact that he had on me, my family, and anyone else whose life he touched and improved is beyond measure. God has blessed me with so many great things, and after His love and sacrifice of His Son Jesus Christ, nothing has been greater than having my Mom and Dad. I will always be grateful for the awesome family and home I was raised in and for the continued understanding and wisdom I gain in my adulthood.

I used to stay at my parent's home the nights before my Dad had dialysis so that I could take him to his early sessions the next day on my way to work. I will always cherish and remember our late night conversations. I would massage his feet to help the circulation or sometimes massage his shoulders to help him sleep better. During this time, Pops would share all kinds of wisdom with me, including stories from his past. Some of our conversations were just about sports or things going on in our lives and the world. God gave us these moments to reinforce the love and bond that was already unbreakable between my Dad and me. I look back at those nights not as time I *had* to take care of my dad but valuable time I *got* to spend with him. Pops instilled two valuable principles that I have tried to live by throughout my adult life. First and foremost, to take care of and think of others before myself because God is taking care of me, and second, to know and get my priorities straight and take care of them. As a youngster, these were two difficult paths to follow. Human nature is to want to take care of ourselves first and enjoy whenever we can, but that is wrong, especially if that comes at the expense of others. My Dad had it correct, and the best part about his advice was that it was Biblical. The Bible is filled with stories about knowing our priorities and taking care of our responsibilities, and the number one moral act that God proclaims for us is to think of and treat others before or as we would ourselves. For it is written:

> The entire law is summed up in a single command:
> "Love your neighbor as yourself."
> (Galatians 5:14)

My Father's love and care for others allowed him to endure and enjoy life as he went through his own health issues. Because he focused on other people's needs over his own problems, Pop's ordeals became less of an issue to him. If you are a parent, you know exactly how this works. Say you had a bad day at work and suddenly your child has some sort of emergency; you drop everything to make sure your child is safe and sound and your bad day almost becomes insignificant. No matter what was going on, my Father did not change his positive attitude and love for life and Jesus Christ. In fact, my Father embraced whatever situation he was in. During good times, like spending family vacations together, it was God's way of blessing him; however, whenever adversity occurred, my Father looked at it as a challenge to persevere and trust in the Lord. It doesn't have to be an emergency or bad event to take your mind off of yourself; it just takes compassion and care for others. Our thoughts and minds can only focus on so many things at once, so when you put God first and have consideration for others, you inevitably don't worry about yourself. The best part is that you don't have to because God takes care of your needs. Pops combined his care for others with a joyful spirit to make every incident simple and less stressful. I am sure his ordeals were painful and trying but because he never showed it or brushed it off as minor, it lessened the stress on us and allowed us to care for him but not worry. To care but not worry about someone or something is very important when it comes to coping in life. Part of this perspective derives from the attitude of trying your best and giving something your best effort. The other part and most important factor is to have Faith. As stated previously, Faith is the simple, but not easy, core of any relationship and especially a relationship with Jesus Christ.

My Father's trust and Faith in the Lord powered him through to his final days. When Pops was in the intensive care unit before he went to Heaven, a nurse told me that he was a special patient and a joy to care for. I asked her to explain, and she told me that she had taken care of hundreds of patients who had a range of emotions, including sadness, anger, fear, and peace. My Father was not only at peace but she said during the night when no one was around, he sounded joyful, talking and laughing in his bed as if he were at a party with friends. A few days before my Father passed, he told me not to worry because he had seen Jesus along with a few of my uncles and his friends who had already gone to Heaven, and they told my Dad that they would come for him in three days. Just as my Dad told me, three days later he went home to Heaven. Similar to the Angel telling my Grandma that she would be back for her, Jesus assured my Father that He would come back for the my Dad. I have heard and read about such stories before but to experience it through my loved ones is truly inspiring.

As God was working through my Dad during his ordeals, He was also blessing my Mom, giving her the strength and ability to coordinate my Dad's hectic schedule while maintaining our house and her beautiful garden. Like Dad, Mom always considered others over herself, and she was a meticulous provider with a tireless work ethic. Her Christmas trees, decorations, and village that brightened our house during the Christmas season throughout the years were tremendous and many family members and friends enjoyed the fruits of her labor. She also loved to work in her yard and garden where countless strangers have enjoyed the views and complemented her efforts. Like Dad, my Mom did not do things for accolades or rewards; rather she always did what was right and just and lived to honor God. She never grumbled or complained about taking care of my Father and even embraced the opportunity to care for a loved one. Being devoted to Christ throughout her life, Mom accepted whatever role she was given and accepted the outcome with grace and dignity. Even when Pops passed on, Mom did not question God's plan or lament her loss. She thanked God for the wonderful life she shared with her husband, reminisced about the good times and blessings we had as a family, and patiently waits for the time when God calls her home too. I am not saying she is bitter and does not want to be here anymore; on the contrary, she enjoys every day and is always in such good spirits. As much as I cherish the time I spent with my Father, I marvel at my Mom's unwavering spirit and determination and truly value the character that both of my parents instilled in me and my siblings. The core values of honoring God, accepting His path for us, and caring for others above ourselves have been the biggest blessings in my life. It has taken a long time for me to develop this perspective, and I continue on this journey every day, which is one of the reasons I wrote this book.

Bruddah Stu

Friends that are very close but not blood related are often referred to as "brothers" within their network of friends. In Hawaii, the slang for brother is "bruddah." My dear friend Stu (the super Raiders fan in white above) was such a good and loyal friend to so many of us that he was affectionately and simply known as "Bruddah Stu" to those fortunate enough to have been his friend.

I met Stu when I was in the sixth grade and he was in the fifth. We shared similar interests in sports, and our friendship grew throughout high school. We played on the same DII basketball team my senior year, and he was one of my favorite teammates. He was a decent player, but it was his positive and unselfish attitude that made him a great asset to our team. Stu did everything with passion and maximum effort and was always honest about his capabilities and the situations around him. I will always remember the night of my last high school game. We lost the championship game, and I was getting on the school bus; as I was walking down the aisle of the bus, I saw Stu sitting in his chair weeping. I asked him why he was crying, and he told me he was sad because he lost his chance for a high school championship. I looked at him and laughed, then told him that he was only a junior, but since I was a senior, I *really* had no chance to get that title. Being the great friend that he was, he looked up from his seat and apologized because he was thinking about himself and not the seniors on the team that played their last high school game. I sat down next to him and told him that it was ok because he was correct, his class was not good enough to win a championship and this *was* his best opportunity! We both got a good laugh at that, and it was true, they were bad the following year. Our friendship continued to grow throughout our adult lives, and I was honored to be the MC for his wedding. We may not have won that high school championship but we did win several recreational basketball league titles with other friends (pictured at the end of this chapter). Through the decades of our friendship, we supported each other in many ways, professionally as well as personally. Stu was a skilled surgeon, and he stitched me up when I had cut my hand pretty badly one night. I provided architectural services for the renovation of his home and so on, but it was not until Stu's biggest challenge that we were able to do the most for each other.

Stu was taken to Heaven in 2014, much too soon for all of us who knew and loved him but in God's perfect timing. Stu was a devoted husband and father, a loving son and brother, and the most loyal and trustworthy friend anyone could have. Stu was kind, considerate, fair, and disciplined. He was a skilled orthopedic surgeon who had a very successful career, but it was his caring nature that really stood out. Like my Father, Stu knew how to enjoy life to the fullest and did so while making sure others were taken care of and putting them ahead of himself. Selfless and humble are two words that describe my friend, and it was his compassion for others that really defined Stu.

When Stu was first diagnosed with cancer, I told him God could heal him and that he needed to accept Jesus as his Lord and Savior. In his humble appreciative manner, Stu thanked me but declined. Even though he was not ready to welcome the Lord into his heart, Stu appreciated my Faith and prayers for him. Stu had tremendous perseverance and did not let his battle with cancer deter his spirit or passion for life. He kept his office open and still performed surgery while going through chemotherapy! When I asked him if he preferred to take a break from working and just take it easy, he told me he had a responsibility to his family, patients, and employees to keep working, and he received strength and encouragement from knowing he was doing a good thing for others. Stu showed unbelievable sacrifice and dedication that inspires me to this day. As time passed and the affliction progressed, Stu started asking me to share reading material with him about Faith and the Lord. It was not a coincidence that when earthly medicine failed to heal Stu, God was able to come to his aid. As the scripture says:

> My power is made perfect in weakness.
> (2 Corinthians 12:9)

Almost three years after Stu got sick, he was put in hospice care at the hospital. He was there for about a week, and it was during that time that he gave me the opportunity to do the best thing I had ever done in my life to that date. I have prayed for many people in the past, but Stu was the first person to ask me to introduce him to the Lord. It started when several of us were in the room and Stu's mom asked me to read some scriptures to him. I was honored that she asked me and relieved that I had brought my Bible. After reading a few scriptures for Stu, I told him that when he was ready to accept Jesus Christ as his Lord and Savior, I would do my best to help him. I will always remember the day that Stu accepted Jesus Christ as his Lord and Savior.

We were in the Hospital on a Saturday when he told me he wanted to welcome Jesus into his heart. I explained to him about the sinner's prayer and the three important steps to receiving Christ. First was to invite and welcome Jesus into your heart, second was to confess and repent of your sins and ask for His forgiveness, and third was to trust in the Lord for everlasting salvation. I did not know if there was a formal prayer so I asked Stu to repeat after me:

Dear Lord,

I welcome you into my heart as my Lord and Savior. With You by my side, there is nothing I should want or need. I confess my sins to You, Lord, and humbly ask for Your forgiveness. I thank You for blessing me with Your grace and guiding me with Your light, and I trust You with my everlasting salvation. In Jesus's Name, we pray.

Amen!

We said our sinner's prayer together and prayed in Jesus's name to fill Stu with the Holy Spirit. Stu thanked me as I left his room that night, and I was convinced that the Lord would be Stu's Savior. I was even more sure and grateful when I visited him the next day. Stu was excited and wanted to share his experience with me. He told me that after he accepted Jesus and went to sleep, Jesus came to him and reassured Stu that He (Jesus) would take care of him and that everything was going to be great. Jesus showed Stu a glimpse of Heaven and assured Stu that he had a place there. Stu was elated and told me he did not know if he was dreaming, but that it felt better than any dream he'd had before. He was ready to go, in fact, he *wanted* to join Jesus in Heaven. What an experience—meeting Jesus and having Him assure you of your salvation. Like the penitent sinner (Luke 23:40–43), Stu received Jesus and put his faith in the Lord for his salvation near the end of his time in this world, and Jesus delivered Stu just as he did the penitent sinner in the Bible. We were able to spend a beautiful day with Stu, and I marveled at the peace and joy he had in preparation of his journey home to Heaven. Ironically, when Stu awoke Monday morning, he was actually disappointed that he was still in this world. In God's timing, He took Stu home later that Monday and lifted Stu's soul to Heaven just as Stu described to me the day before.

Reading scriptures from the Bible for Stu and his family and helping him become a believer in Jesus Christ is one of the best things I have ever done in my life. Introducing Stu to Jesus Christ is one of the main reasons I decided to write this book. I have so many family members and friends that I want to spend eternity in Heaven with after I leave this world. I invite everyone, even those of you I have not yet had the opportunity to meet, to read this book. Hopefully you will enjoy it, but most of all, I hope it inspires you to reflect on your own life and where you want to spend eternity when your brief time in this world passes. Even if you have doubts, or have other beliefs like Stu did when he first got sick, I hope you choose to accept Jesus Christ as your Lord and Savior. It is never too late to become a believer, and better yet, it is never too early. We do not know when our time on earth is up, so do it now; God is there for you 24-7.

Best team and best friends to the end.
Miss you Stu (far right crouching)!

Do You Pray?

Communication is vital in any successful relationship, and it comes in many forms. We send and receive messages daily through conversations, emails, texts, television, the rare-and-special written letter, and many other methods. It is through these messages that we hopefully grow (professionally or personally), and the more we work on our communication skills, the better understanding we achieve with each other. Talking to God is very similar to our everyday conversations with people but with much greater effect. Prayer is the basis for communicating with God, and as a lifelong Catholic Christian, I thought that everyone prayed. As I looked deeper into that perspective, I realized that most people connect prayer with something religious; therefore, if someone does not consider themselves to be religious, they naturally do not think they pray. On the other hand, there are many people out there who pray that might not necessarily have a relationship with Jesus Christ. I do not know where you stand on this matter, but the reality is that everyone prays in one form or another, depending on your interpretation of what prayer is. Like my friend who I mentioned earlier that "hoped" her son was all right when he got injured playing football, she was praying without even knowing it. Prayer is a simple but very powerful proclamation, and when you think of the basis of prayer, it really comes down to two simple gestures—please and thank you.

Think back to when you were a child or how you raise your children. Whenever a child asks for something, they are often asked, "What's the magic word?" And after receiving something, they might be reminded, "What do you say?" As we all know, the "magic word" is *please* and what you say after receiving something is *thank you*. Praying might not be that simple; however, those two statements are the basis of prayer. Whenever we ask for something, the natural emotion that follows whether you realize it or not is *hope*. The magnitude of our request usually determines how much hope we tie to the wish.

A simple request like placing an order at a restaurant might not generate much hope but we still want the order to come out correctly and the food to be tasty. If we are applying for a job or trying to be accepted into college, the hope for success is much greater. Basically, the more important the wish, the more hope is involved. What really distinguishes prayer from normal requests is whom we present our requests to. True prayer occurs when we bring our thoughts and words to God. We often rely on other people when making a request or thank them for things they may do for us; however, that is not the same as praying. A common statement used by believers and nonbelievers alike is "I pray to God." So many people say, "I'll pray for you," and how many of you have used the hands together prayer emoji? When we say these types of things, we should realize that the truest and strongest prayer happens when we are communicating with God. The power to grant wishes or make things happen depends on the person or entity for which the request is being asked. Asking your boss if you can leave work early or asking your Mom or Dad for a raise in allowance is not praying but asking simplistic requests that they have authority to grant. However, praying that a loved one recovers from illness or wishing for an end to this pandemic is truly in the hands of God.

Many meals are preceded with saying grace, which is basically a prayer asking God to bless the food we are about to eat and thanking Him for providing it for us. People of all beliefs say grace before a meal, but my question is who are they saying grace to? If you do not believe in God then grace loses its meaning. Now some people believe there *is* a God but they do not accept Jesus Christ as their Lord and Savior. Their intentions are good; however, their prayer may not reach the intended destination. It is like asking a stranger on the street to give you a raise in your salary. That person may listen to your request and they might even agree with you and want to give you that raise; however, they do not have the capacity or authority to grant your request. The effectiveness of prayer depends on the source or intended target of that prayer. You've probably heard the term "target audience" when it comes to movies and products for sale. It relates to the people or demographic the producer or seller is trying to appeal to. The same practice occurs when we try to communicate with each other. What and how you say something depends on the person you are talking to and the situation you are talking about. The earlier chapter "Your Words" describes that in more detail. When you pray you are having a conversation with God. Nobody should ever pray to another person, as that would be fruitless. Only God has the ability to hear your prayers through your heart and the authority to answer all prayers because nothing is impossible for Him. Think of conversations that you have with people. You more than likely talk to strangers differently than you would a close friend or family member. Usually, the better you know someone, the easier it is to talk to them and the more intimate or private your conversations can be. In a similar way, when you have a relationship with God, it is easier to pray and open your heart to Him. Anyone can pray, and if you need some encouragement, the Bible gives us the Lord's Prayer:

Our Father, who art in Heaven
Hallowed be thy name.
Thy kingdom come, thy will be done,
On earth as it is in Heaven
Give us this day our daily bread
And forgive us our trespasses,
As we forgive those who trespass against us.
And lead us not into temptation
But deliver us from evil.
(Mathew 6:9–13)

This prayer covers the basic ideals for our relationship with God. First, we acknowledge God, His greatness, and His domain in Heaven and on earth. Second, we ask Him to sustain us daily. Third, we ask for forgiveness just as we forgive. Lastly, we ask for His guidance and deliverance to Heaven. Prayer does not need to be elaborate or grandiose as God is not concerned about propaganda and only asks for sincerity. The most important thing to remember is that God hears all of our prayers and He answers all of our prayers. Because He knows our hearts and innermost thoughts and feelings, our prayers do not need to even be spoken aloud. At the same time, it does no good to try to "fool" God with false words or shallow claims. God knows all of our faults and only wants us to repent and be honest about our sins. This fact should bring comfort to you knowing God will forgive you of your sins, no matter how egregious. If anyone has done something they are ashamed of or afraid of what others may think of them, they carry a burden or guilt that can cause anxiety. Confessing to God and repenting our trespasses allows us to relinquish any burdens or guilt and move on in a positive manner. Even if we do not think we are guilty of sin, it is good to ask God to intervene on our behalf.

> Search me, O God, and know my heart;
> test me and know my anxious thoughts.
> See if there is any offensive way in me,
> and lead me in the way everlasting.
> (Psalm 139:23–24)

People think they know what is best for them and go through their daily routines based on their perspective and priorities. They may even pray based on certain outcomes they desire. Sometimes it is a definitive action, such as praying for someone's healing, or it could be praying for something to happen, like getting into a school or getting hired for a job. Ideally, it is best to leave it in God's hands and pray that God leads you to the right path according to His will. God hears all of our prayers, and He answers every one of them. I know you might disagree with that statement because you remember praying for something to happen and it didn't so you think God did not answer your prayer. When we pray for a loved one to get well and they don't, it's easy to say God did not answer our prayers. If you reacted that way, think beyond the rejection of not getting what you asked for. God did hear your prayer, and He did answer it; it's just that the answer was *no*. God answers prayers in three ways: *yes, no,* and *wait* (or not yet). We should all be able to relate to that. If you are a parent and your child asks you if they can have a cookie, the answer might be *yes,* they can have a cookie since they ate all of their dinner. The answer might be *no,* they cannot have a cookie because they did not eat their dinner. The answer might be *wait* until after dinner. The hardest part about praying is that many times, we do not get the outcome we prayed for and therefore we think our prayers were not answered. God understands our hurt and frustration during seasons of anguish, and He wants to encourage us to be determined and to persevere through those times, trusting in His ways through prayer. As the Bible says:

> Be joyful in hope,
> patient in affliction,
> faithful in prayer.
> (Romans 12:12)

That scripture gives us clear and concise directions for navigating through life's ups and downs. First, we can be happy and joyful knowing that God takes care of us and has prepared a place in Heaven for us to be with Him for eternity. Second, this world is temporary, so we need to persevere and battle through the down times when satan tries to break us down. Finally, we need to stay faithful to God through prayer and allow His grace to flow through us so that others can know that Jesus Christ is our Lord and Savior through our words and actions.

It is July 2022 when I write this section, and we are in very trying times. COVID-19 has been devastating the world for almost three years. Inflation and interest rates in America are skyrocketing as supply chains are depleted. What is most concerning is that the moral fabric of our country is under duress as crime is running rampant and senseless mass shootings happen almost daily. Internationally, the war in Ukraine, atrocities in other countries, and natural disasters taking thousands of lives all over the world make it seem like evil is taking over this world. In times like these, when things seam bleak, it is hope for a brighter future that brings us joy. We know that it takes time to heal wounds and turn things around, so we need to be "patient in affliction." Being patient does not mean do nothing. In fact, it takes perseverance, dedication, and effort to overcome trials and tribulations, and the most important action is to be "faithful in prayer."

Skeptics of God will try to use all of the tragedies and evilness going on in this world to chastise God's love and sovereignty for us. They will say if God were real, why would He let such bad things happen. Like I said previously, it is not for us to ask *why*. The Bible describes, through many scriptures, that while we are *in* this world, we should not be *of* this world. Jesus proclaimed this for his disciples as well as Himself:

> They are not of this world,
> even as I am not of this world.
> (John 17:16)

Let me explain the difference; *in* this world describes a physical location, while *of* this world pertains to being in the same spirit of the world. A simple example would be if a nonbeliever walked into a Church, that person would physically be *in* the Church but would not be considered *of* the Church since they do not share the same spiritual bond with the people of that Church. The world originated as a beautiful, peaceful place; however, when satan was cast out of Heaven along with his demon followers, earth became his domain and he defiled it with his lies and deceptions. Satan continues to deceive many of us to try to get us to turn away from God and His righteous ways. Many Christians feel that we are living in the End-Times, described in the Bible as the period before the Lord returns to earth to bring salvation to His followers and defeat satan and evil for eternity. No one knows how long the End-Times will last; however, many of the recent and current calamities are similar to transgressions described in Revelations, the last book of the Bible (notice I said *of* and not just *in*).

The current state of affairs around the world can be quite depressing when you consider all of the bad things taking place in 2022. The future is never known or promised, so more now than ever. The reason this world is full of evil doers that inflict pain and hurt as well as natural disasters that devastate our lands is that satan is at work, trying to get as many people as possible to turn away from God. In times of struggle, it is easy for satan to cast his aspersions against God in the hearts of nonbelievers; that is another reason I am writing to you. It takes Faith and encouragement to defeat satan, and without God, that task is impossible. Many nonbelievers in Christ and Heaven also do not believe in satan and hell, and that is how satan traps them. If you are unaware of danger, you are more likely to encounter it.

Warning signs are posted for our safety to make us aware of potential hazards. When we see a warning sign posted, it is up to each individual to decide how to heed that caution. Sadly, many disregard the warnings and calamity follows. Satan's greatest weapon is deceit, and he has deceived his victims from the start of humanity. It started with Adam and Eve in the Garden of Eden when satan, in the form of a serpent/snake, tricked Eve into taking a bite of the fruit from the tree of knowledge and sharing it with Adam when God clearly instructed them not to eat fruit of that tree. That disobedience was humankind's first sin and occurred because of satan's treachery. Satan hates God and all of His creations so he loathes us because we are God's greatest work and made in His image. Satan tries to ruin people's lives, and more importantly, their souls, with his deceitfulness because he is physically weak and incapable of causing us bodily harm. Instead, he tries to persuade us to harm ourselves by making poor decisions or doing bad things. It is quite basic. If you think something is stupid or bad, most likely you won't do it; however, if you show poor judgement, you will find a way to justify your bad behavior. That is satan's goal—to get us to think evil deeds are not that bad. Temptation is satan's weapon of choice when it comes to deceiving us. When someone says, "Don't tempt me," that usually refers to something that isn't innocent or positive.

Ironically, satan's biggest hoax is to make people think he *doesn't* exist because when you are aware of satan and his plotting, you can avoid him just like you avoid danger—when you heed warning signs. It is a simple paradox. God wants only the best for us, so He wants us to know about Him and believe in Him. Satan wants to destroy us and knows that his only chance to lead us down a path of destruction and condemn our souls to hell is for people to *not* know about him or believe that he exists. Why do you think God is often referred to as "the light of the world" while satan is called "the prince of darkness"? As you know, when we are in a dark place (literally and metaphorically), we need light to show us the way through that darkness. Light will always defeat darkness, and that is true, literally as well as metaphorically. Whenever you turn on a light in a room, the darkness disappears as quickly as the light appears.

The battle between light and dark can also translate as good versus evil when it comes to our actions. Honorable work and positive actions are usually performed in the light. The greater the achievement, the brighter the light, hence the term "spotlight." Evil doings or shameful actions normally occur in the dark so that they can be hidden from others. Even the term "dark secret" refers to a topic or information that is shameful or can bring harm to an individual. Privacy is not the same as a secret, so please do not confuse the two. Satan thrives on secrecy and uses people's unawareness of his presence to condemn their souls. The good news is that when you come to Jesus and have a relationship with Him, you not only learn about His goodness and how to live a happy, healthy, and peaceful life but you also become aware of satan and the reality of hell. Like a warning sign on the road or on a beach alerting of potential hazards, the Bible informs of us of satan's trickery and disdain for God and humankind as well. We have heard the phrase "knowledge is power" and reading the Bible and having a relationship with God gives us ultimate power to defeat satan. The Bible calls our fight against satan spiritual warfare, and Jesus knows we cannot defeat satan alone so He is there to fight for us and assures us of victory over satan when we believe in Jesus as our Lord and Savior.

Put on the full armor of God
So that you can take a stand against the devil's schemes.
(Ephesians 6:11)

You may be wondering what the "full armor of God" is. Ephesians continues describing attributes, such as "the belt of truth," "breastplate of righteousness," "feet fitted with readiness of the gospel of peace," "shield of faith," "helmet of salvation," and "sword of the spirit, which is the word of God," as the full armor of God. Satan is no match for this "armor," and the way to attain it is by praying continually.

And pray in the Spirit on all occasions
with all kinds of prayers and requests.
(Ephesians 6:18)

The guidance to pray on all occasions does not mean literally to pray twenty-four hours a day; rather it means to have a constant awareness of and fellowship with God so that our daily lives are predicated on honoring Him. One way to put on the armor of God is regularly committing our cares to God, asking Him, praising Him, thanking Him for His provision and living in His presence. As noted earlier, praying in its basic format is asking, honoring, and thanking God for anything and everything in our lives. The more we pray and have God in our lives, the stronger our armor is to withstand satan's pursuit and temptations. We all go through issues in life that we need help to get through. God promises to be with us always and though that does not mean a pain free life of luxury, He does provide peace and perseverance to get through and overcome the tough times. Knowing that God hears and answers all of my prayers, even when the answer is *no*, gives me the freedom and confidence to be completely honest with Him. God's love and forgiveness takes away my burdens and guilt while giving me the clarity and strength to help and encourage others during times of need. Even in loss, I overcome grief with the knowledge that God hears my prayers and always has my best interest in mind. We all need someone to talk to and who better than our Creator and Savior?

In July of 2021, while still dealing with the COVID-19 pandemic, a very close and dear friend, Pete, passed away unexpectedly. Pete was unique in so many ways, from his eclectic musical and cinematic tastes to his sense of humor and pride in whatever he did. Pete was a very private person, but he was always generous and giving of his time and resources. He was selfless to a fault and always let others have the "first fruit." Pete dealt with health and emotional issues that were impacted by the loss of his parents several years back and more recently with the stress of the pandemic. None of us was aware of the dire situation he was going through prior to his passing, and Pete's selflessness prevented him from reaching out for help or asking for assistance. It pains me to think that I might have been able to do more for my friend from a physical, emotional, and spiritual standpoint; however, I trust God's plan, and I pray continuously for Pete's salvation. This sort of loss could have nonbelievers asking, "If God is real, why did He let this happen?" On the contrary, only God knew what Pete was dealing with, or suffering through, and it was part of the Lord's all-knowing wisdom to take Pete from this world when He did.

Pete's passing definitely brought sorrow to those who knew and loved him and while satan might try to use that hurt to discourage us in our pursuit to honor God, it has given me further passion and determination to live for God and bring others to Him! I do not ask why Peter passed on; rather I ask what can I do in remembrance of Pete. I want to honor my friend and help others who are struggling in their situations, and I realize my limits and the need for God to guide me to reach my full potential. 2021 was a turbulent and trying year for my family and me, but I do not complain or lament my losses. Living a life that honors God minimizes regret, but it does not eliminate that feeling of remorse completely when we lose someone close to us.

We cannot change the past, but we can try to improve our present and future. The one thing we can do about both the past and present is pray. I pray for people who have passed on like Pete just as much as I pray for you and me. I thank God for the love and memories I shared with family and friends who have passed, and I ask God to bless their souls and give them salvation. Only prayer allows you to ask for anything because God is all mighty and anything is possible with Him. Similar to my trying season of 2003, I accept God's plan for my life and pray for guidance, peace, and wisdom to not just endure but to triumph over adversity. Think if you have ever hoped for something to happen for you or a loved one—that is prayer. The title of this chapter was sort of a trick question but one for you to ponder; rather than "do you pray?" it is more like "how do you pray?"

Our Fantasy Football League, going strong since 1991, lost two dear members in 2021; miss you Pete (standing far left) and Strat (standing second from right).

He Ain't Heavy
He's my Brother!

The statement above is the title and key phrase of a famous song, and it accurately describes how burdens or challenges become insignificant when caring for loved ones. As I have mentioned before, we do not control incidents that occur and what truly defines us is not the actual events but how we respond to them. It is easy to celebrate victories or share during times of abundance. However, when we suffer loss (physical, personal, financial, and so on) we need to do more than just overcome it; we need to persevere and make something positive from that experience. Think of times when you are caring for or doing things for others and you forget about your own situation; that same focus or peace of mind can occur when you focus on God. When you give your life to God, your perspective changes so that if you are going through trials, you do not go through them alone. God is with us always, in good times and bad, and you can trust in His ways no matter what the situation is.

My Brother Stratton (Scratch to his closest friends) was four years older than me, and we were very different in looks and personality. He was tall, thin, and handsome. I am shorter, heavier, and not so handsome. He was very responsible and great with finances, while I am not so mature and definitely not good with finances. Despite our differences, we were very close and our differences complemented each other. In God's perfect plan, we were able to accept each other's personalities and thrive as brothers. He was strong in areas that I lacked and vice versa so that together we could accomplish great things and have a great relationship. Stratton was far from perfect, but he was a great big brother, and he felt the same about me, his "little" brother. In life, especially relationships, it is more important to complement each other's strengths and weaknesses rather than to match them. As an Architect, I understand the use of metal rebar in conjunction with concrete to achieve maximum structural capacity. The rebar is strong in tension but weak in compression, while concrete is weak in tension and strong in compression. Combining rebar and concrete allows the two materials to work together to achieve strengths they could not reach individually. Similarly, God gives each of us talents or strengths that should be used to help others so that together we can achieve things and persevere through things we could not alone. The Bible describes people of the Church similar to parts of a body.

The body is a unit,
Though it is made up of many parts;
and though all its parts are many,
they form one body.
So it is with Christ.
(1 Corinthians 12:12)

The Bible goes into further detail, describing how a hand and an eye (and other parts of the body) are much different but they need each other to make the body whole. This concept is true for the Church when it comes to spiritual gifts and applies to our everyday life as well. Think of your favorite sports team. Each member has certain responsibilities based on their skill set, and the team has to work cohesively to be successful. My brother, my sister Rella, and I have our own similarities and differences; however, we always support each other and have been blessed to be part of a wonderful family unit. God has blessed me with an extended family that includes many friends who are not blood related. Through God and the nurturing of my parents, my siblings and I understand the importance of putting others first. My Pops would always tell me "Always be considerate of others and help them whenever you can and do not be selfish." I have tried to follow his guidance, and I pray for wisdom and strength to serve others and ask God for forgiveness when I fall short. My family, friends, coworkers, and other acquaintances know that I am there for them and willing to help them out no matter the situation.

God knows who and what we need in our lives, even when we don't understand. Stratton always relished the big brother role, and growing up, I did not understand or always appreciate his big brother ways; however, as an adult, I am very grateful for having him be my big brother. Stratton was always responsible and disciplined, and he looked after everyone he cared for, including me, our sister, and other friends and family members. As mentioned previously, Stratton was always good with finances and had a good business sense. Fortunately, he was also generous and giving. If he was bringing food to a party for eight people, Strat would bring enough food for twelve people or more! When our Father went to Heaven in 2010, Stratton took it upon himself to take on the responsibility of making sure the family was ok. He took our family to Yellowstone National Park for a family road trip vacation like my Dad did when we were kids. He also provided for his family and Stratton hosted all of our big family parties after Pops was gone, including my 50th birthday party, my sister's 60th birthday party, and my Mom's 85th birthday party. He also helped out other family members whenever they were in need. Stratton was a great brother, but like all of us, he was not perfect. One of his shortcomings was having a temper, but his biggest flaw was pride. Most people consider pride to be a positive trait, and in some instances, it can be. Pride has sometimes been described with the following acronym: "**P**ersonal **R**esponsibility **I**n **D**aily **E**xcellence." Following that description would have a positive influence on someone's actions; however, pride can also lead to destruction when it is the arrogant, stubborn type of pride that self-centered people have. The Bible warns of the dangers of having this sort of pride.

When pride comes,
then comes disgrace,
but with humility comes wisdom.
(Psalm 11:2)

This scripture not only warns us about having pride but also gives instruction to gaining wisdom, which is to be humble. Stratton experienced the pain of pride and gained wisdom through humility, just as the scripture describes. Stratton had pride, both the good and bad kind. On the positive side, he was determined to provide for his family and do well in his career with honesty and integrity. Stratton had high principles and values, which is good; however, he also put pressure on himself to maintain that high standard, and he often expected others to have those same standards as he did, and that was bad. He worked tirelessly at the different jobs he succeeded in during his adult life, and he did so on his terms, not relying on shortcuts or "favors." Stratton relied on his intelligence and personality to achieve both professional and financial success. Unfortunately, while Stratton was generous and giving to a fault, he was bad at asking for help for his own needs because he did not want to burden anyone. This form of pride was detrimental to both his mental and physical health.

Stratton had type 2 diabetes, and due to complications from this disease, battled many health issues. He had very poor circulation that led to neuropathy (numbness, muscle weakness, and pain). In 2019, he cut his elbow and contracted a staph infection that landed him in the hospital. He needed surgery and heavy antibiotics to kill the staph and save his arm. Because his kidneys were already under stress from the diabetes, the massive doses of antibiotics damaged his kidneys to the point of dialysis. My Father was on dialysis for about three years before he passed and for the most part, got through his sessions quite smoothly and had very little complications after them. My brother was completely opposite. Dialyses sessions were uncomfortable for Stratton, and he suffered excruciating pain throughout his body a few hours after each session. In addition to dialysis, Stratton sustained several other injuries and incidents that were beyond his control. It was a long and difficult season for my brother; however, he endured as best he could, and I saw a transformation in him that was heartbreaking and heartwarming at the same time.

Stratton dealt with his numerous ailments for over a decade; however, we were not aware of the severity off his illness because he kept it to himself. He would always tell me not to worry and that there was nothing they could do to help his condition, so he would just have to deal with it. In hindsight, that was not true; it was just his way of dealing with it. I get frustrated and sad sometimes when I think I could have done more to help my brother but then I put my faith in the Lord, and He gives me peace knowing Stratton is in Heaven with God and Pops.

As mentioned previously, conflict causes strife. Stratton's conflict was that while he needed assistance with his health issues, his pride prevented him from asking for help because he did not want to be a burden. Stratton was a very caring person and this may sound strange but I would tell him he cared too much about some things. He was always well dressed and took great pride in his appearance. We had totally different perspectives on this topic. I remember when we were young adults and were getting ready to go play basketball. He told me he had to find a shirt that matched his shorts, and I told him it did not matter if they matched. He told me, "You gotta look good to play good." I laughed and said, "It's not how you look, it's how you play." This is a sample of what I mean when I say he cared too much about some non-important things.

Stratton's main conflict was that he was used to being independent, hardworking, and able to provide for his family, but when his health declined, it was difficult for him to accept his situation. I mentioned earlier how important our words are. When Stratton was younger and working absurd hours, he would tell me he could not wait to retire so he would not have to go to work. Then when he was forced to retire and had to drive to dialysis, he told me he wished he was back at work and did not have to go to dialysis. I told him not to wish for things of the past but cherish the present and be grateful he could drive to dialysis. It was sad to see my brother's health deteriorate, but I am grateful that as his body weakened, his spiritual strength grew. Many things happen in our lives that we do not understand, but Faith in God gives us to power to *accept* situations and appreciate everything God gives us, even if it seems negative. Stratton would ask me why he was suffering through so many ordeals and if he was being punished for past transgressions. I told him the story of Job. If you know the Bible, you know the story of Job (pronounced jōb), if you do not know the Bible, then that is another reason you should learn it; learn it, don't just read it. I told Stratton that when ordeals happen, I do not ask God *why* because that would show a lack of Faith, and I would not understand His reason even if He gave me one. Instead, I ask God *what*; as in what would You have me do God? Or what can I do to make it better? We have to learn to accept things and trust in the Lord rather than lament and complain. The serenity prayer asks for God's guidance and help in times of duress.

God grant me the serenity to accept things I cannot change, the courage to change the things I can, and the wisdom to know the difference.

I encouraged my brother and reassured him that the more he trusted God, the less he would have to understand, and more importantly, the less he would worry. I told Stratton that because God is in control of my life, I *care* but I do not *worry* about issues that present themselves. My brother put aside his own pride and priorities and gave everything to God, and I saw a humble side of my brother that allowed himself to be vulnerable and at peace with his situation. Stratton truly endured much pain, and it was through God's blessings that my brother found the strength to persevere. It is so easy for people to thank God and sing His praises when things are going well, but it is true Faith and Belief in Jesus as our Lord and Savior to sing His praises and thank Him for His blessings during trials and tribulations. My brother lived a good but much too short life and though we went to Church from the time we were children and were raised as Catholic Christians, I believe he was at his spiritual strongest when his health faded and he lost his previous lifestyle. I say Stratton's life was much too short, but that is my own selfish opinion because I love him and miss him so much. The real truth is that Stratton's life was however long it was supposed to be according to God's perfect plan, and though I miss my brother dearly, I do not ask God why He took Stratton so soon. Instead, I ask God what I can do to atone for my sins and make this world better until I am called home to Heaven like Stratton was.

My big brother loved to teach or impart wisdom to those he cared for and would often justify his actions as "teaching moments," whether he was right or wrong. As we grew to be adults, the lessons for me were fewer but he always had my best interest in mind and wanted the best for all of his loved ones, especially his wife Brenda and son Skyler. Of all of the lessons that Stratton taught me, I admire his perseverance through adversity. Perseverance is one of the most valuable characteristics a person can have. We admire those who "never give up," and we have all heard the saying "no one likes a quitter." There is a big difference between *quit* and *surrender*, especially when it comes to our Faith in God. When you have Faith in the Lord, you *surrender* yourself to Him without question, not just in good times or when you get what you want but more so during trials and hard times. Surrendering yourself to God means allowing Him to lead you in your words and actions, regardless of the situation. While many people quit on God when they are suffering, the encouraging news is that God never quits on us! He is always there, even if we do not think He is. Our pride gets in the way sometimes and we think we know what is best and can control our lives. When you give yourself to the Lord, you realize how little you actually control, and that is when you let Jesus take the wheel. Stratton surrendered his soul to God, and the Lord blessed him as the Bible promised.

Blessed is the man who perseveres under trial,
because when he has stood the test,
he will receive the crown of life that God has promised
to those who love Him.
(James 1:12)

Stratton lived in Las Vegas, and every time I had to leave to come back home to Hawaii, instead of saying *goodbye* to Stratton, I would tell him *see you later* because I told him that would be true, whether I saw him in Vegas again or when I see him in heaven. When God took Stratton to Heaven on November 20, 2021, he looked so peaceful and all of his pain had been taken away. Stratton taught me so much growing up and even through his passing; like my Pops, he is an inspiration and strong motivation for me writing this book for you. When I brought Stratton's ashes from Vegas to Hawaii, my buddy Gregg (below, second from left) asked if the ashes were heavy, and the perfect response was "he ain't heavy, he's my brother." See you later, Scratch!

My brother Scratch (sitting) fought the good fight until God called him home, and Craig's shirt (far left) says it all!

Believe

My sis believed in her dream
of owning the best show dog in the state.

Think of this worldly example. Imagine the best resort in the
world. A place that was beautiful in appearance, with the best
of everything, luxurious accommodations, world-class dining,
awesome entertainment and activities, and all the enjoyment
you can imagine. The owner and creator of this wonderful
place welcomed all of his family and friends and others
he knew to stay there for free for as long as they pleased;

however, if the owner did not know you, you were not allowed to enter. It did not matter how wealthy, powerful, or famous you were or even how good, charitable, or caring you were. If you did not know the owner, you could not enter this wonderful place. It did not matter if you knew his name; you needed to have a relationship with him. If you had a personal and caring relationship with him, the owner would put your name on his guest list so that when you showed up to enter this beautiful place, you would be welcomed with open arms. If you did not know him and your name was not on the guest list, you would be denied entry. To make things easier for you, the Owner sent you an open invitation to meet and get to know him so that when the time came, your name would be on the guest list and he would recognize you as one of his companions. If this place existed and you had the chance to meet the owner, I am sure you would take advantage of that opportunity.

Heaven is incredibly better than this place, and God is the almighty Creator and Keeper who loves us and wants us to join Him there. Heaven is so pure and beautiful that sin and sinners are not allowed to enter. That is why God sent His one and only Son Jesus Christ to pay for our sins. God knows that alone we cannot defeat satan, but with God's grace and mercy guiding us, satan does not stand a chance. You would think that with so much at stake and so much to gain, it would be difficult to attain the level of goodness and purity to enter Heaven; however, God wants us to join Him, so He makes it simple and provides us with perfect directions to reach that destination. When I say simple, I do not necessarily mean easy. In fact, I think the hardest part is the starting point. You have to *believe* in God and Jesus Christ, which means believing in someone and something that occurred thousands of years ago. Even the Bible recognizes how difficult it is to get people to believe in the Lord our God.

But if serving the Lord seems undesirable to you,
then choose for yourselves this day whom you will serve,
whether the gods your forefathers served beyond the river,
or the gods of the Amorites, in whose land you are living.
But as for me and my household, we will serve the Lord.
(Joshua 24:15; italics mine)

Serving the Lord starts with accepting Jesus Christ as your Lord and Savior and welcoming Him into your heart just like my buddy Stu did. The first step is to acknowledge Him; the second step is to *believe* in Him. Like I mentioned in a previous chapter, it starts with your words and is followed by your actions. It might be easy for you to say the words but you have to truly believe with all of your heart so that your actions match your words. Many people have heard about God, even satan knows that God is real, but if you have not welcomed God into your heart and accepted Him as your Lord and Savior, you are at risk of falling into satan's traps. Satan is envious of God and is the one who causes destruction in hopes of luring you away from God. Belief in something is a person's greatest conviction.

When you believe something or in something, that will affect how you live your daily life. Almost everything that we do on a daily basis is based on our beliefs. A simple task, such as picking out your clothes for the day, is based on the belief that the attire is appropriate for the activities of that day. Changing someone's mind depends on the topic and how strong the belief is for that person. Believing in something usually relates to a topic or lifestyle that most likely cannot be proven with logic and facts. Belief starts with having Faith, and as mentioned at the beginning of this book, that means believing in something that is not seen or cannot be proven with logic. Believing in something certain or factual is not having Faith. Something like gravity occurs whether you believe in it or not. If you fall out of a building, you will come crashing down, regardless if you believe in gravity or not. Mathematically, one plus one equals two in any country or language, and that does not change no matter what the belief of that country is. Believing in Jesus Christ and having a true relationship with God gives you strength, wisdom, and peace to overcome anything, especially satan's temptations. It does not promise a life without trials and tribulations, but it does assure us of perseverance and salvation in all seasons. The Bible relates a relationship with God as the following:

He will be like a tree planted by the water that sends out its
roots by the stream. It does not fear when heat comes;
its leaves are always green. It has no worries in a
year of drought and never fails to bear fruit.
(Jeremiah 17:8)

Another beautiful aspect of believing in God is that He is unchanging and unwavering, so you can trust His words and actions in all circumstances. It is ironic that people have a hard time believing in the truest thing in the world (this time I said *in* the world; notice the difference). Knowing God's Word and living to honor Him gives believers clarity and vision without having to worry about what the world thinks. Society is filled with many people who live in fear, all types of fear, and this fear is debilitating because it can cause anxiety that leads to physical, mental, and emotional destruction.

I think one of the biggest fears people have is the fear of missing out (FOMO). They fear of missing out on anything from activities to financial gains to almost anything else you can name. This fear is based on a lie that if you miss out on something, your life will be lacking. Lies are also a tactic that people living in fear use to either get or not lose possessions. People will go through all sorts of elaborate schemes to keep up with a lie. I have done that in the past, and I regret it. It is much better to be honest and straightforward. The beautiful thing about telling the truth is that you do not have to worry if anyone believes you because it does not matter. The truth remains the same whether people believe it or not. That is why I am comfortable writing to you. I am sharing the truth with you, and it is up to you to accept it or not. Jesus was very clear about His truthfulness and how important it was to know Him if we wished to go to Heaven.

> I am the way and the truth and the life,
> No one comes to the Father except through me.
> (John 14:6)

You might be asking, "If God wants what's best for us, why doesn't He just defeat satan and make everyone be good and obedient to Him?" The answer is that God wants us to choose Him and to come to Him of our own free will. Think of it this way. The best relationships in this world are the ones we *choose* to be in. I am pretty sure that you have heard the saying "you can't pick your family, but you can pick your friends." That adage runs deeper than just for family and friends; it relates to other relationships as well (work, play, romantic, and so on). Basically, the key element of *choice* comes into play. All relationships are better when the parties involved *want* to be together rather than *have* to be together. It is sort of like the difference between a *job* and a *hobby*. A job is something you are paid to do or have to do (like household chores), while a hobby is something you are willing to pay to do or want to do for free.

We are all God's children, and He loves and cares for all of us; however, not everyone reciprocates those sentiments toward God. God wants us to have a relationship with Him, but we have to make the choice to come to Him. You know that if you want something in this world, most times you need to go out and work for it. There is usually a process to accomplish things or receive rewards. Most of us work and receive paychecks every two weeks for work done during that pay period. Sports championships are won at the end of grueling seasons. Graduations occur when we complete required courses. Many of these accomplishments take perseverance and hard work. The energy and will to work through setbacks comes from the belief that the goal is attainable. You need to believe you can succeed in something to make it happen, and the more you believe in something or love something, the stronger your conviction is for it and the more you are willing to sacrifice for it. God's belief and love for us is so great that He sacrificed His only begotten Son for us. As one of the most famous scriptures says:

> For God so loved the world
> that He gave His one and only Son,
> that whoever believes in Him
> shall not perish but have eternal life.
> (John 3:16)

We need this kind of belief in the Lord to overcome the perils of this world. There is suffering in our lives and much evil in this world because satan is roaming the earth, causing death and destruction. I keep saying that we need to believe to achieve. On the other hand, if you do not believe in something that does not mean it does not exist or can't harm you. Many of us need to see something to believe it exists, or we need "proof" to believe it is real. Sadly, your belief, or more importantly, nonbelief has no impact on the reality of something or someone's existence. The sun's ultraviolet rays are an example of what I am talking about. We cannot see the rays with our naked eyes, and many people do not believe the rays can be harmful to our health so they go to the beach or out in the sun for extended periods of time with insufficient protection (clothes, sunscreen, and so on). Their nonbelief in the harmful rays does not prevent them from getting sunburn, or in some cases, skin cancer.

Not believing satan and Jesus are real because you cannot see them or do not have scientific evidence or proof of their existence does not change the fact that they are both very real. The difference is in each of their intent. God wants to save our souls and give everlasting salvation, while satan wants to corrupt and condemn your soul. There are things that we cannot see but we can feel, such as wind. We all appreciate a cool breeze, and sailboats rely on wind to move. You do not need faith for wind to exist, and you cannot affect the wind or influence its impact on the world by your beliefs. Wind can be helpful (cooling areas or providing energy) but can also be destructive (tornados and hurricanes), regardless of our beliefs. It is a fact that everyone believes in something. Even scientists cannot prove everything and need to believe in conclusions or hypotheses that have no factual evidence. I asked my friend Hugh, who is a smart, scientific guy, what the sun is made of, and he told me it was made of hydrogen and helium. I then asked him if anyone has samples of the sun, and he said no. He told me studies of the sun came to that conclusion. Basically, they *believe* it is made of hydrogen and helium. There are so many things in this world and our daily lives that we accept without absolute proof or facts, yet many find it difficult to believe in God.

Thankfully, God is patient and will be there whenever we call on Him. The penitent sinner (Luke 23:39–43) and my buddy Stu were able to accept God into their hearts in their final hours, and God gave them eternal salvation and a place with Him in Heaven. As I said many times before, God knows our hearts, so while it is not enough to just say you believe in God, it is one of the first steps to take in your journey to salvation. You do not need to make any grand gesture or proclamation to accept Jesus as your Lord and Savior; it just takes honest conviction. It also does not matter if you think you are good enough or deserve God's love. You just need to confess and repent of your sins and ask God with a humble heart to be your Lord and Savior.

Everyone who calls on the name of the Lord will be saved.
(Romans 10:13)

Any successful person will tell you that a big key to success or victory is determination. This means always trying and never giving up. The fuel for this determination is the same as the fuel to get to know God—*belief*! Believing in a cause, a goal, and yourself allows us to overcome obstacles and achieve great feats.

My sister Rella loves animals, especially dogs. At a young age, she got involved with dogs, shows, breeding, obedience training, and anything else related to that sport. My sister did not have the advantages of other more affluent competitors, but she believed in her dogs, and more importantly, she had Faith that God would work things out according to His plan. Through many years of dedication, hard work, love for her dogs, and mainly belief in God's plan, Rella was rewarded with numerous relationships and experiences, and in 2011, her Vizsla Cooper won the award for being the number one all breed conformation show dog for the State of Hawaii. To be perfectly honest, my brother and I never dreamed Rella would achieve that award, but we were so grateful that her belief and God's plan proved Stratton and me wrong. Rella is a glowing example of believing in something and having the dedication to see it through no matter how daunting the task is. One reason Rella is able to persevere and succeed when the odds were stacked against her is her belief and Faith in the Lord. She graduated from a Catholic high school and that Christian foundation has grown through her adult life.

Winning and achieving earthly rewards are great and there is nothing wrong with believing in yourself to accomplish such feats; however, it is so much greater when we put our Faith in God and live to honor Him. Having that belief and living for Jesus will reward you with eternal salvation in Heaven when your time on earth is done. It will also make your days on earth better as well. If someone has good health, financial wealth, or professional success, people might say they are blessed; however, they do not say that about people dealing with health, financial, and professional problems. The truth is that they both could be blessed, just not in worldly terms. A true believer in God knows that every day is a blessing, regardless of the situation. Faith and belief support will and determination, which allow us to overcome great adversity. We can all agree that there is much suffering in this world, especially during the pandemic, and many have perished unfairly; however, we must do our best to overcome the hardships. Believers in Christ can draw on His strength for guidance and assistance because when you live for God, you become more than just yourself. The Holy Spirit is in you and helps you through the tough times. Alone, we as individuals might be able to do small tasks; as a group or team, more can be accomplished; with God, we can achieve anything! When it comes to salvation, the Bible declares:

> Jesus looked at them and said,
> "with men this is impossible,
> but with God all things are possible."
> (Mathew 19:26)

It does not matter how rich or successful you are on earth or even how kind and generous you are (although those are Godly characteristics) because, as the Bible says above, humans cannot win or earn entry into Heaven. It is only with and through God can anyone enter heaven. There are so many ways to dedicate your life and honor God, and He has given each of us unique gifts to share with others as blessings; however, you have to *believe* in Jesus as the first step to unleashing His strength in you. With the spirit of the Lord in you, you will be able to endure and overcome any obstacle, hardship, or loss. I am not saying you will never suffer or have bad times; on the contrary, sometimes those with strong Faith suffer the most, as satan knows he cannot defeat God so he attacks the most dedicated followers of Jesus. As I have mentioned previously, through trying times, it does no good to ask *why*, as in "why me" or "why did this happen." That shows a lack of Faith, and you won't get an answer you can understand. Instead, ask God *what*, as in "what would you have me do" or "how can I serve you best." Give your burdens to God and ask Him to guide you through the storm so when adversity strikes, He will give you the strength to persevere and the passion to inspire others. With belief in God, you can achieve great things!

And made it a reality
through belief and perseverance!
(Rella with John, who handled Cooper
during his 2011 championship campaign)

Let's Go!

Everything in this life and in this world has a beginning and an end, a start and a finish. Some events are distinct and foreseen in there duration, like the hours in a day. Sometimes the outcome is predetermined, like the ending of a movie, and sometimes the outcome is unknown, like the result of a competitive contest. The more uncertainty there is in the outcome, the more interest and involvement occurs. Spectators are limited to what they can do or what impact they have on the event they are watching. Participants, on the other hand, can influence or impact the event in ways (positive or negative) that affect or even determine the outcome. Think of something in your life that you partake in. It can be something that you enjoy, like exercising, or something you might not enjoy, like exercising. You set the time or duration of the activity and the goals for the outcome. Sometimes one dictates the other, and sometimes they are one in the same. Let's use running as an example. You can set a certain distance as the goal and forget about the time it takes to run that distance or you can set an amount of time you want to run while not caring about the distance. Sometimes both the time and distance are the goals, such as a marathon runner trying to complete the full course within a certain timeframe. Regardless of the situation or activity, all of the things we participate in have some similarities.

Life itself is the biggest event of all, and everyone participates whether they want to or not. No individual should be put above the good of the team. In society, we all depend on one another to contribute in some way or another. As bad as the world seems now in 2022 (sorry, I know I am taking long to write this book.) it would be much worse if we did not work together as best we can. Unfortunately, too many people are not helping, and worse, some are a detriment to the well-being of others. Criminals are obvious menaces to society and make life difficult for others, but it is not just criminals who need to repent and change their ways. A much larger number of people, Christians and non-Christians alike, need to help or need help to cope during these trying times. We all have burdens, and a relationship with God does not prevent trials and tribulation but it does provide a source of strength and encouragement to persevere. It all starts with accepting Jesus Christ as your Lord and Savior. That is only the beginning. Consider this parable.

Listen! A farmer went out to sow his seed.
As he was scattering the seed, some fell along
the path, and the birds came and ate it up.
Some fell on rocky places, where it did not have much soil.
It sprang up quickly, because the soil was shallow.
But when the sun came up, the plants were scorched,
and they withered because they had no root.
Other seed fell among thorns, which grew up and
choked the plants, so they did not bear grain.

Still other seed fell on good soil.
It came up, grew and produced a crop, multiplying
thirty, sixty, or even a hundred times.
(Mark 4:3–8)

The seed is the Word of the Lord. People who do not accept the Word are like the seed that fall on the path, and satan is the bird who devours it. The next group of people is like the seed that fall on rocky places. They get excited quickly but not sincerely for Jesus, so their commitment is shallow and as soon as temptation or trials hit them, they wither. The third group of "seed" wants to follow Jesus; however, they have so much going on around them, they cannot dedicate themselves and are choked by their own "thorns." The seed on "good soil" are those who accept Jesus Christ as their Lord and Savior and cultivate that relationship so that they can live a rich and rewarding life in the Lord. Take a moment to consider if you fall into one of these categories. The good news is that we have the opportunity to correct or improve our relationship with God, or better yet, start one if you don't yet have one. Unlike people, God does not hold grudges and is always there for us with open arms no matter how bad or how often we have failed Him. We need to confess and repent of our sins with a sincere heart and God will welcome you home like the Prodigal Son (Luke 15:11–32). If you are not familiar with this parable, that is another reason to read the Bible.

I guess you could consider this book a type of "seed" being sown to you at this moment. Hopefully, it reassures believers but more importantly, gets nonbelievers to accept the Lord. I started this chapter by talking about a beginning and an end to everything. To finish or accomplish anything in this world, you need to start that task, project, and so on. The previous chapters talked about different people and life experiences that God has blessed me with. They are all part of this great journey for me; this book itself is a meaningful piece of my life, and I hope that when my time in this world comes to an end, God will be pleased with me and welcome me home to Heaven. It has taken me a long time to finish this book but as I get closer to completing it, I realize that I had to *start* writing for it to become a reality. What has been the most amazing part about writing this book is that although my intentions are to encourage anyone reading it, whether they accept God, be better people, or just get them through the day, writing this book has actually helped me with my day-to-day life and the realization of how important God is in my life. Knowing that God is real and loves me allows me to live in complete peace and confidence. I am not bragging or saying that I am invincible, but I do not fear or worry, as the Bible reassures us.

> The Lord is my light and my salvation—
> whom shall I fear?
> The Lord is the stronghold of my life—
> of whom shall I be afraid?
> (Psalm 27:1)

When Stratton was in the ICU a few days before his passing, we were in his hospital room the entire day (Wednesday, November 17, 2021). We were not wearing masks the whole time, and I even swabbed his chapped lips with water and put my face right up to his to try and hear him speak. As we were coordinating with the staff to determine what hospice facility he would be transferred to, we were informed that the patient down the hall passed away from COVID-19. I felt bad for that family as they mourned the passing of their loved one. What was odd about the situation was that most of the family members were not wearing masks. What was disturbing was that the nurses on the floor were going in and out of that room and in and out of my brother's room without any regard to the fact that the other patient had COVID-19. When they transferred Stratton to the hospice facility on Thursday, November 18, we were informed that he tested positive for COVID-19 (not surprising). My family and I were then tested, and we all tested negative. I was literally inches from my brother's face without a mask so I know God was protecting us. It is this kind of strength and fearlessness that God provides to those who trust in His ways.

Living for God also gives you a sense of purpose and clarity during good times and bad. Allowing God to guide you will always get the best results. As I mentioned before, we are not in control of our lives but we can control some things. We can control our *effort* and our *attitude*. When you focus on giving great effort and having a great attitude in everything that you do, you will soon realize that success and achievements are not just recognized by end results. You can "win" by more important measures, such as how you treated others. Ironically, if you give good effort and have a good attitude, end results actually become less significant. When you believe in God and have a relationship with Him, earthly rewards pale in comparison to your treasures in Heaven. I just recently got the opportunity to practice what I preach. I have been working for the City and County of Honolulu for the past three years under contract and this past week, interviewed for a permanent position. The interview went well, and I was selected for the position; however, while the permanent position gave me job security, it also came with a significant pay *cut*. My initial reaction to the situation was that it was unfair; however, I am at peace with it because I had been praying about it and asked God to put me where He wanted me to be. I told my bosses during the interview that I would always give good effort and have a good attitude and, no offense to them, it was not because of them. In fact, I told them about my Faith and how I lived to serve the Lord and not humankind. As the Bible says:

> Whatever you do, work at it with all your heart,
> as working for the Lord, not for men.
> (Colossians 3:23)

I know the Bill of Rights declares "separation of Church and State," however, that does not pertain to an individual's Faith and even more so, our moral responsibility. The Bible talks about how satan roams this world and tries to pull us away from God, and the current state of the world appears to back up that decree. There is a saying, "It is never the wrong time to do the right thing." Now is the best time to accept God into your life because we never know when our time here is over. It is never too early to start getting to know God and when you make that decision, I have good news and bad news for you. The "bad news" is that alone, you will never be perfect or even "good enough" to get into Heaven. The "good news" is that when you give your life to Jesus, He will cleanse you of your sins and prepare a place for you in Heaven so you do not have to do it alone. What we do on earth matters, and while we need to live with compassion and generosity, God will take you to the next level, literally! I mentioned God's grace and mercy numerous times in this book and for those of you wondering what I mean by that, simply put *grace* is getting blessings that we have not earned or do not really deserve, while *mercy* is not getting the punishment that we truly deserve for our sins. Like a parent who loves and cares for their child, God loves us and cares for us. When a parent disciplines the child, it is to protect the child from greater harm in the future. Similarly, God wants us to avoid the punishment of hell. When we welcome Him into our hearts, we can live by the fruits of the spirit.

> But the fruit of the Spirit is love, joy, peace, patience, kindness, good, faithfulness, gentleness, and self-control. Against such things there is no law.
> (Galatians 5:22–23)

The fruits of the Spirit are listed in such a way that every three reflect a different perspective. The first three, *love, joy,* and *peace,* are blessings God gives to us. The second three, *patience, kindness,* and *goodness,* are blessings that we should show others. The final three, *faithfulness, gentleness,* and *self-control,* are what we need to have in ourselves. Living with all nine attributes will lead to a truly wonderful life for us and those we encounter. The world is full of challenges and even with the fruits of the Spirit, there will be down seasons and doubtful moments.

Another strength the Bible talks about that is just as important as the nine fruits is *perseverance,* which is the ability to endure hardships and thrive during trials. My buddy Gregg told me this riddle: How does the Opihi (a shellfish that lives on rocks along the Hawaii coastline and gets pounded by the waves) get big? He *holds on!* That is a simple yet not so easy task when the ocean waves come crashing down on you but the Opihi must do that if they want to survive. Similarly, we, too, must hold on when things get difficult. Fortunately for us, God is there to provide strength, wisdom, and reassurance to get through the tough times and be better people for it. Everyone needs help or support during their lives, and we usually ask those closest to us for assistance when we need it. Our family and friends know and love us, so they are the ones we can depend on. God is the only one who truly knows us inside and out, and He cares and loves us more than any friend we have. Ask yourself this, would any of your friends sacrifice their child for you? Of course not, that would be unheard of, but God did that for you and me when he sent Jesus to sacrifice Himself on the Cross for our sins! You might not be able to visually see God but there are many visible examples of His work in action. When you open your heart to Him, you will be able to hear Him in your soul. What is even more amazing is that God sees and hears you and me *all the time.* It does not matter where you are or how alone you think you are, God is there and knows what you are thinking and more importantly, what is in your heart. Knowing He is with you should give you confidence to accomplish great things in His name, humility to make wise decisions with a pure heart, and strength to persevere during trying times.

The key to all of this comes down to the simple decision of accepting Jesus Christ as your Lord and Savior, but that is just the start. I accepted Jesus as my Lord and Savior when I was baptized as a child; however, I continue to have a lifelong relationship with Him. I know I have failed Him many times, but thankfully, He has not and will not ever give up on me. As I have shared my experiences with you, I know 100% that it is all part of God's perfect plan for me to have lived, loved, and lost according to His will. Even writing this book is in His plan for me, and it was His plan for you to read it. Like every great journey or any undertaking we choose to accept, it has to start with our decision to go for it, followed by some sort of action. You have taken the first step by reading this book. Whether you are already a believer needing reinforcement, a person on the fence about your beliefs, or even a nonbeliever just looking for encouragement during these trying times, God brought this book to you for a reason, and I am glad that He did. The stories and words along with the selected scriptures are from my heart and meant to appeal to everyone but especially those who doubt or question God's presence. Reflect on your own experiences and see how any of this relates to you.

So what are you going to do next? Every day is an opportunity to make your life and the lives of those around you better. We also have the chance to strengthen our relationship with God (or start one if you don't have one). It takes both words and actions to accomplish anything, so whatever you decide to do today, think about what impact it will have on your life and the lives of your loved ones. Then figure out how to achieve your goals, and finally, put your plan into action. The shoe brand Nike used to have a slogan, "Just Do It," telling people to stop procrastinating and to get out and be active. In life, it takes more thought and planning depending on the task. As I mentioned at the beginning of this book, the more important the outcome, the longer and harder we are willing to work to achieve our goals. Heaven is a place God has prepared for us to spend eternity with Him after our time on earth is done. It is our choice to accept and welcome Him into our hearts but it takes a lifetime to fulfill. Once you start something, keep going and build momentum. If you are ready to accept Jesus as your Lord and Savior, I am happy for you. Find a good Bible-based church to take the next step and pray to God for guidance. If you are not ready yet, I still thank you for reading this book and allowing me to share my life with you. Before I go, I just have one last question for you. When you pass on from this world, where do *you* want to go? I want to go to Heaven, and the only way to get there is by having a relationship with Jesus. Don't wait; it is never too soon to accept Jesus into your heart. Let's go!

Band of brothers, play on!
L-R: Gregg, Coy, Stratton, Hugh, Lax (me)

Words to Encourage

Use the guidance below to encourage yourself and those around you.

- God is good all the time; all the time God is good.

- Don't *B-lame*, don't Blame!

- Find solutions to problems, not excuses for mistakes!

- Don't ask *why* bad things happen. Ask *what* can I do to make things better.

- Don't say you *have* to do something; say you *get* to do something. It does not change the task, but it will change your attitude.

- You control your *effort* and your *attitude*, so make sure both are good and you will be fine.

- Care for others and you will not have to worry about yourself.

- Whether you say you *can* or you *can't*, you are correct, so use positive words.

- It is important to know the difference between *quit* and *surrender*.

- Alone, we can achieve a little bit; with help from others, we can achieve a little more; with God, we can achieve anything!

- Win each day!

About the Author

Layton Pang's life experiences have allowed him to enjoy, persevere, and inspire others to live in faith, hope, and love regardless of the situation. Layton is an architect and wrote this book for everyone and anyone needing encouragement or guidance.

Printed in the United States
by Baker & Taylor Publisher Services